DICTIONARY OF SHIPPING TERMS

By

PETER R. BRODIE, F.I.C.S.

D1354830

|L|L|P|

LONDON   NEW YORK   HAMBURG   HONG KONG
LLOYD'S OF LONDON PRESS LTD.

1985

Lloyd's of London Press Ltd.
Legal Publishing and Conferences Division
26–30 Artillery Lane, London E1 7LX

U.S.A. AND CANADA
Lloyd's of London Press Inc.
87 Terminal Drive, Plainview
New York, NY 10003 USA

GERMANY
Lloyd's of London Press
P O Box 11 23 47, Deichstrasse 41
2000 Hamburg 11, West Germany

SOUTH EAST ASIA
Lloyd's of London Press (Far East) Ltd.
903 Chung Nam Building
1 Lockhart Road, Wanchai
Hong Kong

British Library Cataloguing in Publication Data
Brodie, Peter R.
　　Dictionary of shipping terms.
　　1. Shipping—Dictionaries
　　I. Title
　　387.5′0321　　HE567

ISBN 1–85044–069–7

Text set in 9 on 11pt Linotron 202 Ehrhardt
by Wyvern Typesetting Ltd., Bristol
Printed in Great Britain by St. Edmundsbury Press, Bury St. Edmunds

PREFACE

Shipping covers a wide range of activities and the international movement of goods by sea is generally achieved only by virtue of the contributions of a number of people: shipowners, tramp and liner operators, shipbrokers, freight forwarders, ship's agents, loading brokers and many others as well as the importers and exporters who provide the cargoes.

There is a tendency for each of the activities to be performed by specialists and it is the purpose of this *Dictionary* to give a better understanding of the terminology of the others. It is hoped that this book will be of particular use to students of shipping and those entering the profession.

London, 1985   P.B.

To
I.B. and S.J.B.

A

a/a *see* **always afloat.**

a.b. *see* **able seaman** *below.*

able seaman seaman who is qualified by examination and length of service at sea. Often abbreviated to **a.b.**

A.B.S. American Bureau of Shipping—American ship classification society. *For the functions of a ship classification society, see* **classification society.**

abt. about. For example, a telex containing an offer for the charter of a ship might describe her as abt. 2,500 tonnes DWCC.

a/c account. This abbreviation is used when referring to a bank account, for example a **current a/c** and when allocating costs, such as in the phrase **for the a/c of charterers.**

accept except term used by either the shipowner's broker or the prospective charterer's agent during the negotiations for the charter of a ship to signify that an offer or counter-offer is accepted apart from certain clauses or details. These are then listed together with the amendments sought.

accomplish a bill of lading (to) to surrender an original bill of lading to the carrying ship at the discharge port in exchange for the goods. If more than one original bill of lading has been issued, only one need be surrendered to the ship, the others becoming non-negotiable.

accomplished bill of lading original bill of lading which has been surrendered to the carrying ship at the discharge port in exchange for the goods.

act of God occurrence over which there is no human control, such as an unusually severe storm or lightning strike, resulting in a loss. Generally, contracts of carriage contain a clause excluding the carrier from liability for any such loss. It would not be an act of God, however, if the loss could reasonably have been foreseen or avoided.

ad val.   ad valorem.

ad valorem freight   freight calculated on the value of the goods, expressed as a percentage thereof.

addcomm.   *see* **address commission.**

addendum (to a charter-party)   clause, or set of clauses, attached to a charter-party and incorporated into it.

additional demurrage   amount of money paid to the shipowner by the voyage charterer, shipper or receiver, as the case may be, for failing to complete loading or discharging before the agreed period of demurrage has expired. The daily rate of additional demurrage is agreed in the charter-party.

additional freight   extra charge imposed in accordance with the contract of carriage by a shipping line on the shipper, receiver or bill of lading holder, as the case may be, for additional expenses incurred in discharging the cargo. This charge generally applies when the port stipulated in the contract is inaccessible or when to discharge there would result in an unreasonable delay to the ship: under these circumstances, the shipping line may have an option under the contract of carriage to proceed to another port to discharge the cargo where extra costs may be incurred.

address commission   commission payable by the shipowner to the charterer, expressed as a percentage of the freight or hire, often 2½ per cent. Although this commission was sought by charterers as a means of reducing the freight or hire, these are capable of being adjusted by the shipowner to allow for it.

adjustment   calculation of a loss by an average adjuster. In the case of general average, the adjustment sets out all the contributions of the parties who had an interest in the marine adventure.

admissible as general average   said of an expense which is recoverable in a general average adjustment from all the parties to the marine adventure. Whether or not a particular expense is admissible depends on the rules or jurisdiction agreed in the contract of carriage. The York–Antwerp Rules state, for example, that the expenses of entering and leaving a port of refuge are admissible as general average. Also referred to as **allowable as general average**.

advance call   payment, normally made once a year in advance, by a shipowner to the protection and indemnity association with which his ship is entered. This payment is the basic fee for the service provided by the association and is based on the ship's tonnage. The total of members' calls represents the anticipated amount of claims against the association's funds.

advance freight   freight payable at a time, agreed by the shipowner and the shipper, before the goods are delivered at the place of destination in the contract of carriage.

advance on freight   money advanced by the shipper to the master of a ship to pay for his disbursements while in port. It is often repaid by deduction from freight.

advance to master   money advanced to the master of a ship by the charterer to pay for his disbursements while in port. It is often repaid by deduction from freight or hire money.

advice note   note sent by a supplier of goods to, for example, a ship's port agent, giving a description of the goods, the date on which they are due to arrive and the method of despatch.

affreightment   the hiring of a ship.

aft   at or towards the stern or rear of a ship.

after peak tank   small tank situated at the extreme after end of a ship. It normally holds water ballast and is used to help to trim the ship, that is, to adjust the draughts forward and aft.

agency clause   clause in a charter-party which stipulates whether the ship's agents at the loading and discharging ports are to be nominated by the shipowner or the charterer.

agency fee   fee payable by a shipowner or ship operator to a port agent whose duties may include arranging a berth with the port authority, ordering pilots, tugs and labour, entering the ship in at Customs and collecting freight.

agent   widely used short form for ship's agent. *For definition, see* **ship's agent**.
   as agent only   form of words used with a signature to a charter-party or bill of lading to indicate that the party signing is doing so merely on behalf of a principal, whether it be the master, owner or charterer of the ship, and has no rights or liabilities under the contract of carriage.

aground   touching the bottom.

A.H.R.   Antwerp–Hamburg range. *For definition, see* **range of ports.**

air draught   (1) the maximum height from the water-line to the topmost point of a ship, that is, the superstructure or the highest mast. This information is required for ships having to navigate bridges. It is important for a ship operator to be certain which definition, this one or the one immediately below, applies to an air draught quoted to him.

air draught   (2) the clearance between the topmost point of a ship and a bridge. It is important for a ship operator to be certain which definition, this one or the one immediately above, applies to an air draught quoted to him.

air draught   (3) maximum height from the water-line to the top of the hatch coamings. This information is necessary in some bulk trades where loading is effected by conveyor belt which projects over the hatchway. The ship must be low enough in the water, if necessary by retaining sufficient ballast on board, to allow the conveyor to clear the hatch coamings.

all in rate   freight rate which is inclusive of all surcharges and extras.

all purposes   time allowed in a voyage charter for loading and discharging combined, expressed as a number of days or hours. Also referred to simply as **purposes.**

all time saved   term used in a voyage charter-party to define one method by which despatch money is calculated, that is, by deducting time used for loading and/or discharging, as the case may be, from a theoretical time up to the expiry of laytime which includes excepted periods. For example, a charterer may be allowed 10 laydays for loading. He calculates the expiry of laytime taking account of excepted periods, such as week-ends, and arrives at a theoretical number of calendar days, say 15. Should he only use four laydays to load, he is entitled to 11 days' despatch money. *See* **laytime saved** *for an alternative method of calculating despatch money.*

allotment (of wages)   allocation by a seaman of a percentage of his wages on a regular basis to named persons.

allotment note   document in which a seaman gives authority to the master or owner of a ship to allocate a percentage of his wages on a regular basis to named persons.

allowable as general average   said of an expense which is recoverable in a general average adjustment from all the parties to the marine adventure.

Whether or not a particular expense is allowable depends on the rules or jurisdiction agreed in the contract of carriage. The York–Antwerp Rules state, for example, that the expense of entering and leaving a port of refuge is allowable as general average. Also referred to as **admissible as general average.**

always afloat   term in a charter-party which stipulates that the charterer must not order the ship to a port or berth where she would touch the bottom.

American Bureau of Shipping   American ship classification society. *For the functions of a ship classification society, see* **classification society.**

amidships   at or in the middle of a ship.

Amwelsh   voyage charter-party, whose full name is the Americanized Welsh Coal Charter-party, used for shipments of coal from the United States of America.

anchorage   place where ships drop anchor, away from shipping lanes, to wait until a loading or discharging berth becomes available, or to take bunkers from a bunker barge, or to discharge cargo to barges, or when laid up.

anchorage dues   charges imposed by a port authority on ships anchoring at or off the port.

angle of repose   angle formed between the horizontal and the slope made by a bulk cargo such as grain or iron ore. The smaller the angle, the more likely a cargo is to shift.

annual survey   examination of a ship undertaken in dry dock by a classification society surveyor. This survey is carried out at intervals of about 12 months for the purpose of maintaining class in accordance with the rules of the classification society.

any time day or night   term used in a time charter-party to signify that the shipowner may deliver the ship or that the charterer may redeliver the ship, as the case may be, at any time of the day or night and not necessarily during normal working hours.

a.p.   (1) *see* **all purposes.**

a.p.   (2) additional premium.

a.p.s.   *see* **arrival pilot station.**

a.p.t. *see* **after peak tank.**

arbitrate (to) to determine a dispute between the parties to a charter-party, bill of lading or any form of contract by means of arbitration. *See also* **arbitration** *below.*

arbitration method of settling disputes in private by means of one, or more than one, arbitrator. Arbitration is thought to be quicker and less costly than going to court. Arbitrators are lay people, and charter-parties often stipulate that they be commercial or shipping men whose direct experience is a further reason for arbitration as opposed to litigation. There is a tendency, however, towards professional arbitrators.

arbitration award decision by an arbitrator or arbitrators as to which party to the contract is responsible in the event of a dispute.

arbitration clause clause in a contract, such as a charter-party, which stipulates that any dispute between the parties arising from the contract be resolved by arbitration. The clause also specifies the place where the arbitration is to be held, the number of arbitrators and their qualifications, and the procedure should one party fail to nominate an arbitrator.

arbitrator person who is nominated to settle a dispute arising from a contract. He or she may be a professional arbitrator or a commercial person. Shipping contracts often stipulate that, in the event of a dispute, the arbitrator appointed must be a commercial person or a person experienced in shipping.

area differential element in the freight of a shipping line or liner conference which reflects the additional costs of serving a particular area.

arrest (of a ship) seizure of a ship by authority of a court of law either as security for a debt or simply to prevent the ship from leaving until a dispute is settled.

arrest a ship (to) to seize a ship by authority of a court of law. *See also* **arrest (of a ship)** *above.*

arrival pilot station location often used as the place of delivery of a ship by the shipowner to the charterer at the commencement of a time charter. The hire charge commences from the time of arrival unless the ship arrives prior to the first of the laydays. In such a case, the hire charge commences at the beginning of the first layday or sooner at the option of the charterer.

arrived ship requirement of all voyage charters that the ship must have arrived before laytime can commence. Where a berth or dock has been nominated by the charterer, the ship must have arrived at that berth or dock. When a port is nominated, the ship must have arrived at the port although various legal decisions have defined differently a port in this context in cases where there is no berth available and the ship is obliged to wait.

articles of agreement written agreement between the master of a ship and the crew concerning their employment. It includes rates of pay and capacity of each crewman, the date of commencement of the voyage and its duration. The agreement is also known as **ship's articles**.

a.s. alongside.

as is in the condition in which the subject-matter is. This expression is used when goods, or a ship, are offered for sale without repair or rectification.

as is, where is in the condition in which the subject-matter is and at the place where it is lying. This expression is used where goods, or a ship, are offered for sale without repair or rectification and with delivery to the purchaser being at the place where the goods are lying.

asphalt tanker ship specially designed for the carriage of asphalt. This is carried in the ship's large centre tanks. This cargo must not be allowed to come into contact with water and, for this reason, water ballast may not be carried in the centre tanks but only in the wing tanks.

astern at or towards the stern or rear of a ship.

a.t.d.n. *See* **any time day or night**.

athwartships across the ship, that is, from side to side. Said of cargo stowed in this way, as opposed to lengthwise.

a.t.s. *See* **all time saved**.

Austral voyage charter-party devised by the Chamber of Shipping of the United Kingdom and the Australian Grain Shippers' Association and used for shipments of grain from Australia. The full name of this charter-party is the Chamber of Shipping Australian Grain Charter.

Austwheat voyage charter-party devised by the Australian Wheat Board and the Chamber of Shipping of the United Kingdom and used for shipments of wheat and flour from Australia. The full name of this charter-party is the Australian Grain Charter.

autonomous port   type of port in France which is self-funded and managed by a council made up of representatives of the municipality, dock workers and others.

average   term used in marine insurance to mean a loss which may be general (*see* **general average**) or partial (*see* **particular average**).

average (to) (laytime)   as a voyage charterer, to offset the time used in loading cargo against that used in discharging for the purpose of calculating demurrage or despatch. If, for example, a charterer earns five days' despatch at the loading port but there is a period of three days' demurrage at the discharging port, the charterer has a net claim for two days' despatch money.

average adjuster   expert whose services are used by insurance underwriters to calculate complex marine insurance claims or who, in the case of general average, is appointed by the shipowner to determine the contributions due from all the parties to the voyage.

average bond   statement signed by cargo interests undertaking to pay their contribution to general average and/or salvage as well as any special charges determined by the average adjuster. Cargo interests also undertake in this document to provide documentation showing the value of the goods to enable the adjuster to calculate the contribution. This bond is required in consideration of the release of the goods.

average guarantee   statement signed by insurance underwriters guaranteeing to the shipowner that they will pay the contribution due from cargo interests to general average and/or salvage as well as any special charges determined by the average adjuster. Without this guarantee, cargo interests are required to pay the shipowner an appropriate sum of money in consideration of the release of the goods.

B

b.   bale. *For definition, see* **bale (capacity)** *below.*

back load   load which enables a vehicle to return loaded to the place or country from where its previous load came. Also referred to as a **return load**.

back to back charter   contract between a charterer and a sub-charterer whose terms and conditions are identical to the contract, known as the head charter, between the charterer and the shipowner. The purpose of agreeing identical terms is to ensure that any money for which the charterer may be liable to the sub-charterer, for example, despatch money, is recoverable from the shipowner.

backfreight   freight payable to a shipowner for the carriage of goods back to the port of loading or to another convenient port when the vessel is unable to reach the port of destination because of an excepted peril or because the consignee fails to take delivery of the goods or provide instructions for their disposal.

b.a.f.   bunker adjustment factor. *See* **bunker surcharge**.

bale (capacity)   total cubic capacity of a ship's holds available for the carriage of solid cargo which is not capable of filling the spaces between the ship's frames. It is expressed in cubic feet or cubic metres.

ballast   heavy weight, often sea water, necessary for the stability and safety of a ship at sea which is not carrying cargo. Such a ship is said to be steaming **in ballast**.

ballast (to)   to steam between two ports without a cargo. Reasons for a ship having to ballast include: (a) no further cargo being available at the port where the ship is discharging; (b) in some trades, a ship may perform a series of voyages between two ports with a (suitable) cargo available in only one direction; (c) in other trades, it may be more economical to steam empty to a port to pick up a lucrative cargo than to take low-paying cargo to that port.

ballast bonus   sum of money paid by a time charterer to a shipowner in recognition of the fact that the shipowner is unlikely to find a cargo near to the place of redelivery of the ship at the end of the period of the charter and is therefore obliged to ballast his ship elsewhere.

ballast leg   sub-division of a ship's voyage during which the ship is not carrying a cargo. It is useful for a shipowner or ship operator to separate this part of the voyage from loaded legs in order to evaluate the profitability of the voyage and to assess requirements for bunkers since a ship may consume less when in ballast.

Baltcon voyage charter-party devised by the Baltic and White Sea Conference and used for shipments of coal from the United Kingdom to Baltic, Scandinavian and White Sea ports. The full name of this charter-party is the Baltic and White Sea Conference Coal Charter.

Baltic and International Maritime Conference association whose main object is to promote and defend the interests of shipowners. It also has a membership of shipbrokers and has been responsible for contributing to the creation of a large number of charter-parties and other shipping documents.

Baltic Mercantile & Shipping Exchange institution, located in London, England, also known as **the Baltic Exchange** or simply **the Baltic**, whose main function is to provide facilities for the chartering of ships by its members: chartering agents, acting on behalf of charterers, negotiate with shipbrokers who represent shipowners on the "floor" of the Baltic. Other activities include air chartering, future trading and sale and purchase of ships.

Baltime general purpose time charter-party published by the Baltic and International Maritime Conference (B.I.M.C.O.).

Baltimore Form C voyage charter-party used for shipments of grain from the United States of America. Its full name is the Approved Baltimore Berth Grain Charter Party.

banana carrier ship specially designed for the carriage of bananas. Bananas ripen quickly if not maintained at the correct temperature which is achieved by ventilating with cold air.

bar sand-bank which forms at the mouths of rivers and which very often limits the type of ships which are able to reach up-river destinations. In many cases, ships have to lighten, that is, to discharge some of their cargo to barges or small ships, before being able to navigate over a bar and complete the voyage. Equally, ships loading at an up-river port may only be able to load part of the cargo, the balance being taken on board after the ship has cleared the bar.

bar draught depth of water at a bar, that is, a sand-bank which forms at the mouths of rivers.

bareboat charter (1) the hiring or leasing of a ship for a period of time during which the shipowner provides only the ship while the charterer provides the crew together with all stores and bunkers and pays all the operating costs. This type of charter is favoured by persons or companies who wish to own a ship for investment purposes but who do not have the desire or expertise to operate the ship. Similarly, it is favoured by persons or companies who have a particular requirement for a ship and the expertise with which to operate one but without the wish or ability to purchase. A ship hired out in this way is said to be **on bareboat charter**. Also referred to as a **demise charter** or a **charter by demise**.

bareboat charter   (2) abbreviation for bareboat charter-party. *For definition, see* **bareboat charter-party** *below*.

bareboat charter (to)   to hire or lease a ship for a period of time during which the shipowner provides only the ship while the charterer provides the crew together with all stores and bunkers and pays all the operating costs. Also known as **to demise charter** and **to charter by demise**.

bareboat charterer   person or company who charters a ship for a period of time, provides crew, bunkers and stores and pays all operating costs. Also known as a **demise charterer** or **charterer by demise**.

bareboat charter-party   document containing the contract between the owner of a ship and the demise charterer, and signed by both, in which are all the terms and conditions such as the period of the charter, the rate of hire, the trading limits and all the rights and responsibilities of the two parties. Also referred to as a **demise charter-party**.

Barecon 'A'   standard bareboat charter-party published by the Baltic and International Maritime Conference (B.I.M.C.O.).

Barecon 'B'   standard bareboat charter-party used for newbuildings financed by mortgage, published by the Baltic and Maritime Conference (B.I.M.C.O.).

barge   flat-bottomed vessel mainly used on rivers and canals. Some types are self-propelled while those which are not are towed or pushed. Barges are often linked together and towed in a line known as a string.

barge (to)   to send (cargo) by barge.

barge-carrying ship   ocean ship which carries barges. These barges are loaded with cargo, often at a variety of locations, towed to the ocean ship, sometimes referred to as the mother ship, and lifted or, in some cases, floated on board. After the ocean crossing, the barges are off-loaded and towed to their various destinations. The ocean ship then receives a further set of barges which have been assembled in readiness. This concept was designed to eliminate the need for specialized port equipment and to avoid transhipment with its

11

consequent extra cost. One example of barge-carrying ships are the L.A.S.H. (lighter aboard ship) ships.

barratry negligence or fraud on the part of the master or crew of a ship resulting in a loss to the owners of the ship or her cargo.

base cargo (1) relatively dense cargo stowed at the bottom of a hold to provide a ship with stability when at sea.

base cargo (2) minimum quantity of cargo required by a shipping line to make it worthwhile to call at a particular port for loading.

base rate basic rate of freight of a shipping line or liner conference on to which are added, or on which are calculated, the various surcharges such as the currency adjustment factor or bunker surcharge.

batten down the hatches (to) to place wooden battens over the edges of a tarpaulin which goes over the hatch beams used to cover a hatchway.

b.b. below bridges.

bdl. bundle.

beam the maximum breadth of a ship. This is sometimes a factor in determining whether a ship is suitable for a particular port: in some cases, a ship may be too wide to pass through a lock; in other cases, the outreach of cargo-handling equipment may not be sufficient to reach the centre of the hatchway which is sometimes a requirement when discharging bulk cargoes.

bearer (of a bill of lading) person who tenders the bill of lading to the ship at the place of discharge in exchange for the goods. Bills of lading are often made out **to bearer**.

Beaufort Scale scale of wind forces. The figures in brackets represent wind speeds in knots.

0	Calm	(less than 1)
1	Light air	(1–3)
2	Light breeze	(4–6)
3	Gentle breeze	(7–10)
4	Moderate breeze	(11–16)
5	Fresh breeze	(17–21)
6	Strong breeze	(22–27)
7	Moderate gale	(28–33)

8	Fresh gale	(34–40)
9	Strong gale	(41–47)
10	Whole gale	(48–55)
11	Storm	(56–63)
12	Hurricane	(64–71)

bends   *see* **both ends.**

berth   place alongside a quay where a ship loads or discharges cargo or, in the case of a lay-by berth, waits until a loading or discharging berth is available. This term is also frequently used to signify a place alongside a quay each of which is capable of accommodating only one ship at a time.

berth (to)   to moor alongside a quay.

berth charter-party   charter-party in which a particular berth is nominated by the charterer. The time allowed for loading or discharging, as the case may be, does not start to count until the ship reaches the berth.

berth standard of average clause   clause in a charter-party setting out the contribution to be made by the charterer to any claim for loss or damage to cargo for which the shipowner is liable.

berth terms   expression signifying that the contract of carriage is subject to the customs and conditions of the ports of loading and discharging.

b.h.p.   brake horse power.

bilge   area at the lower part of a hold where liquids collect and are pumped out at regular intervals.

bill   widely used short form for bill of lading. *For definition, see* **bill of lading** *below.*

bill of health   written statement by the authorities at a port that those on board a ship are in an acceptable state of health to make physical contact with the shore.

bill of lading   document issued by a shipowner to a shipper of goods. It serves as a receipt for the goods, evidence of the contract of carriage and document of title. As a receipt, it contains the description and quantity of the goods as well as suitable notations if the goods are not in apparent good condition when received by the ship. As evidence of the contract of carriage, the bill of lading contains the terms and conditions of the contract or, where the contract is represented by a charter-party, a reference to the charter-party. As a document of title, the bill of lading is used by a third party to take delivery of the goods from the ship.

bill of lading to order   bill of lading which requires an endorsement by the consignee before goods can be delivered to him by the carrying ship.

Bimchemvoy   standard voyage charter-party used for the carriage of chemicals in tankers, devised by the Baltic and International Maritime Conference (B.I.M.C.O.).

Bimchemvoybill   bill of lading intended to be used for shipments of chemicals in tankers under the Bimchemvoy charter-party.

B.I.M.C.O.   *see* **Baltic and International Maritime Conference**.

Bimcosale   standard bill of sale published by the Baltic and International Maritime Conference (B.I.M.C.O.), used in the purchase of ships.

Biscoilvoy   standard voyage charter-party used for shipments of vegetable and animal oils and fats, published by the Baltic and International Maritime Conference (B.I.M.C.O.).

Biscoilvoybill   bill of lading intended to be used for shipments of vegetable and animal oils and fats under the Biscoilvoy charter-party.

b/l   *see* **bill of lading**.

black list   list of countries published by a particular government which will not allow ships to trade at its ports if they have traded at ports in the countries on that list.

black products   crude oils, such as heavy fuel oils. Also referred to as **dirty (petroleum) products**.

Blackseawood   voyage charter-party used for shipments of timber from the U.S.S.R. and Romanian Black Sea and Danube ports, published by the Shipchartering Co-ordinating Bureau, Moscow.

Blackseawoodbill   bill of lading intended to be used for shipments of timber from U.S.S.R. and Romanian Black Sea and Danube ports under the Blackseawood charter-party.

bleeding wing tank   tank, one of which is situated at each side of the top part of the hold of a bulk carrier. It is designed to carry free-flowing cargoes such as grain, acting as a division at the top of the stow to reduce shifting of the cargo while at sea. The cargo contained in these tanks is bled into the hold before being discharged. When not carrying cargo, this tank may be used for water ballast.

block stow (to)   to place cargo in the hold of a ship in stacks of even length with no pieces protruding so as to make the most efficient use of the space in the hold.

block stowage   the placing of cargo in the hold of a ship in stacks of even length with no pieces protruding so as to make the most efficient use of the space in the hold.

blt.   built.

b/n   *see* **booking note**.

boat note   receipt given by the ship for goods loaded on board.

boatman   person who attends to the mooring and unmooring of ships.

bollard   post, fixed to a quay or ship, for securing mooring ropes.

bonded store or bonded warehouse   enclosed place, under the control of Customs authorities, where the imported goods which are stored there are not subject to duty until they are removed by the importer.

book space (to)   as a shipper or his agent, to reserve space in a ship for the carriage of certain defined goods from a place of loading to a place of discharging.

booking   reservation made by a shipper or his agent with a carrier for the carriage of certain defined goods between defined places.

booking list   list, compiled by a shipping line or its agent, of all cargo bookings for a particular sailing.

booking note   document containing the terms and conditions of a contract between a shipper and a shipping line for the carriage of goods on a particular ship between specified ports or places.

both ends at both loading and discharging ports. This term is often used together with n.a.a.b.s.a. (not always afloat but safe aground), with o.s.p. (one safe port), with o.s.b. (one safe berth) and to qualify the prices of bunkers on delivery and redelivery in a time charter. Often abbreviated to **bends**.

both to blame collision clause clause in a bill of lading or charter-party which stipulates that, in the event of a collision between two ships where both are at fault, the owners of the cargo must indemnify the carrying ship against any amount paid by the carrying ship to the non-carrying ship for damage to that cargo. This clause arises because, under American law, a cargo owner is not able to make any recovery from the carrier for damage resulting from negligent navigation but may instead sue the non-carrying ship which in turn seeks recovery from the carrying ship in proportion to its fault. This would render a carrier indirectly liable for a loss for which he is not directly liable to the cargo owner. The clause has, however, been held to be invalid in the American courts when incorporated into a contract with a common carrier.

bottle screw device which applies tension to ropes or chains used for lashing cargo. Also referred to as a **turnbuckle**.

bottom the hull of a ship or the ship itself. When a movement of cargo is effected in, say, two bottoms, it is divided for shipment in two ships or sailings.

bottom stow cargo goods which are stowed at the bottom of a ship's hold because of their relatively high density and the probability that they would damage other goods if stowed elsewhere.

bottomry the borrowing of money by the master of a ship using his ship as security. Also called a bottomry loan. The document in which the ship is pledged is known as a **bottomry bond**.

bow curved forward part of a ship.

bow door watertight barrier which seals an opening in the forward end of a roll-on roll-off ship through which rolling cargo is wheeled or driven along a ramp into or out of the ship. This door is often made up of the ramp itself which is operated hydraulically.

bow ramp inclined plane which connects the forward end of a roll-on roll-off ship to the shore or quay on which rolling cargo is wheeled or driven into or out of the ship. The ramp is very often designed to make a watertight door to cover the opening in the ship.

bow thruster   small propeller near a ship's stem which is used for better manœuvrability at low speeds.

box   widely used term to signify a shipping container. *For definition, see* **container**.

box hold *or* **box-shaped hold**   hold of a ship which is square or almost square in shape. Ships so constructed normally have wide hatchways to enable cargo to be lowered directly into the desired position in the hold.

box rate   rate of freight per shipping container, as opposed to per tonne or per cubic metre. Since a box rate is unaffected by the actual quantity loaded into the container, it is in the shipper's interest to load as much cargo as possible, subject to the maximum allowed, to effectively reduce the cost of carriage for each tonne or cubic metre.

brackish water   fresh water mixed with sea water, having a density between 1,000 and 1,026 kilogrammes per cubic metre.

break bulk (to)   to commence to discharge a bulk cargo. It is sometimes a condition of a contract of carriage that freight, or some percentage of it, becomes payable on breaking bulk.

breakbulk   relating to dry cargo lifted on and off ships one piece or bundle at a time by means of cranes or derricks, but not shipped on trailers or in shipping containers. Such goods may be described as **breakbulk cargo**; the ships which carry them are sometimes referred to as **breakbulk ships** which, if operated on a regular basis between advertised ports, provide a **breakbulk service**. Also referred to as **conventional**.

Britcont   (1) voyage charter-party published by the Chamber of Shipping of the United Kingdom.

Britcont   (2) bill of lading published by the Chamber of Shipping of the United Kingdom.

broke (to)   to negotiate the terms for the charter of a ship.

broken stowage   allowance made for space lost in a ship's hold by reason of the irregular shape of a cargo.

brokerage   fee or commission payable by a shipowner to a shipbroker for the successful negotiation of a charter. It is normally expressed as a percentage of the freight or hire. Brokerage may or may not be payable, according to the terms of the charter-party, should the voyage or period of the charter not be completed.

Brussels Tariff Nomenclature   tariff system, adopted by many countries, which classifies all commodities carried from one country to another, for Customs purposes. It is the basis for the tariffs of many shipping lines. Each commodity has a unique code known as a **B.T.N. number**.

b/s   *see* **bunker surcharge**.

bs/l   bills of lading. *For definition, see* **bill of lading**.

b.t.   *see* **berth terms**.

B.T.N.   *see* **Brussels Tariff Nomenclature**.

bucket elevator   moving belt which brings a continuous supply of buckets loaded with bulk commodities, such as coal, to a point over the open hatchway of a ship and then empties them into the hold.

bulbous bow   rounded projection at the forward end of a ship which reduces water resistance, thus allowing an increase in speed when the ship is in ballast.

bulk cargo   homogeneous unpacked dry cargo such as grain, iron ore or coal. Any commodity shipped in this way is said to be **in bulk**.

bulk carrier   single deck ship designed to carry homogeneous unpacked dry cargoes such as grain, iron ore and coal. Such ships have large hatchways to facilitate cargo handling. Often referred to as a **bulker**.

bulk container   shipping container designed for the carriage of free-flowing dry cargoes such as sugar or cereals. These are loaded through hatchways in the roof of the container and discharged through hatchways at one end of the container by tipping.

bulk discharge open top container   shipping container designed for the carriage of bulk cargoes such as coal. The top is open enabling cargo to be loaded from the top by conveyor or grab and is covered by waterproof sheeting while in transit. The cargo is discharged through a hatchway in one end of the container by tipping.

bulker   *see* **bulk carrier**.

bulkhead   separation between compartments in a ship which may be trans-verse (from side to side) or longitudinal (running along the length of the ship). Bulkheads contribute to the structural strength of the ship and prevent the spread of fire or sea water.

bulk-oil carrier   *see* **ore/bulk/oil carrier**.

bulk-ore carrier   ship designed to carry ores, having wide hatchways and a high centre of gravity. The holds are self-trimming, that is, they are shaped in such a way that the cargo levels itself. This makes such ships suitable for the carriage of grain.

bunker (to)   to call at a port for the purpose of taking on bunkers.

bunker adjustment factor   *see* **bunker surcharge**.

bunker broker   intermediary in the negotiations between an oil company and a shipowner or ship operator for the purchase of bunkers.

bunker deviation clause   clause in a voyage charter-party permitting the shipowner to proceed to any port on or off the route to take on bunkers.

bunker escalation clause   clause in a voyage charter-party which states that, although the charter has been concluded on the basis of a particular price for bunkers, if a higher price is paid for bunkers used during the contracted voyage, the shipowner is to be reimbursed for the extra cost by the charterer.

bunker surcharge   extra charge applied by shipping lines and liner con-ferences to reflect fluctuations in the cost of bunkers. This surcharge is expressed either as an amount per freight ton or as a percentage of the freight. Also referred to as a **bunker adjustment factor** or **fuel oil surcharge** or **fuel adjustment factor**.

bunkering port   port at which a ship calls to take on bunkers.

bunkers   a ship's fuel.

buoyage   the provision of buoys to mark a channel or to alert shipping to dangers, wrecks or other obstructions.

Bureau Veritas   French ship classification society. *For the functions of a ship classification society, see* **classification society**.

butane carrier   ship designed to carry butane in liquid form. The butane is carried in tanks within the holds; it remains in liquid form by means of pressure and refrigeration. Such ships are also suitable for the carriage of propane.

B.V.   Bureau Veritas—French ship classification society. *For the functions of a ship classification society, see* **classification society**.

C

c.a.b.a.f.   *see* **currency and bunker adjustment factor.**

cable ship   ship designed to carry, lay and repair submarine cables.

cabotage   (1) coasting trade, that is, the movement of cargoes by ship between ports on the same coast or between ports of the same country.

cabotage   (2) reservation of the coasting trade of a country to ships operating under the flag of that country.

c.a.d.   *see* **cash against documents.**

c.a.f.   *see* **currency adjustment factor.**

call   (1) visit of a ship to a port for whatever reason, for example, to load or discharge cargo, to take on bunkers or to land an injured crewman.

call   (2) amount levied by a protection and indemnity association against its shipowning or ship operating members. The total of calls paid to the association represents the total of claims made against its funds together with its own operating costs during a 12-month period. This total is estimated by the association and payments in advance, known as advance calls, are levied against members. If this proves insufficient, further payments, known as supplementary calls, are levied. Each member's contributions are based on his ship's tonnage.

call forward (to) (cargo)   as ship's agent at the port of loading, to instruct the shipper or consignor to deliver the goods to the ship at a certain time on a certain date for loading.

call forward (to) (vehicles)   as ship's agent at the discharge port, to instruct the receiver or consignee to bring his vehicles alongside the ship at a certain time on a certain date in order to take delivery of the goods.

call rate amount of money payable by a shipowner to the protection and indemnity association with which his ship is entered, for each ton of the ship's tonnage.

call sign sequence of letters and numbers, unique to each ship, by means of which ships can be identified when being contacted by radio.

calling-in-point place where a ship is required to report when passing, for example, to a port authority when approaching the port. Also known as a **reporting point**.

canal transit dues charge levied by a canal authority, such as that for the Suez Canal, for transiting. This charge is based on the ship's tonnage.

cancellation (of a charter) repudiation of the contract, most often by the voyage or time charterer when the ship misses her cancelling date, or by the time charterer when the ship is off hire for more than the period stipulated in the charter-party.

cancelling clause charter-party clause specifying the last date, known as the cancelling date, on which a ship must be available to the charterer at the agreed place. If the ship arrives after the cancelling date, the charterer may have the right to cancel the contract.

cancelling date last date, agreed in a voyage or time charter-party, by which a ship must be available to the charterer at the agreed place at the commencement of the contract. If the ship is not available by that date, the charterer may have the option to cancel the charter.

capacity plan document detailing the capacities of all the cargo spaces of a ship and all the tanks used for oil fuel, diesel oil, lubricating oil, fresh water and water ballast. The capacities are expressed in cubic feet or cubic metres and, in the case of the tanks, the quantity in tons or tonnes which they can hold.

captain title given to the master of a merchant ship.

car carrier ship designed for the carriage of cars. Dual purpose ships are often employed in this trade, carrying cars on the outward leg and bulk cargoes, such as ore or grain, on the return leg. For this purpose the ships have car decks

21

which are hoisted clear by means of winches so that there are no obstructions for the bulk cargoes.

car deck deck of a ship on which cars are carried. In dual purpose ships, when carrying a bulk cargo, the car decks are hoisted clear or folded against the sides of the ship.

careen (to) to repair, clean or paint the hull of a ship.

cargo (1) goods carried in or on a ship.

cargo (2) cargo interests, such as the shipper or receiver. This term is used when distinguishing between cargo and ship, for example, concerning costings or contractual responsibilities.

cargo battens strips of timber fixed to the frames of a ship, often horizontally but sometimes vertically, to keep cargo away from the sides of the ship, avoiding damage and condensation. Also known as **spar ceiling** and **permanent dunnage**.

cargo plan plan, in the form of a longitudinal cross-section of a ship, drawn up before loading commences, on which are shown the possible locations in the ship of all the consignments taking into consideration their port of destination and their safety in transit as well as the safety of the ship. A cargo plan is often taken to be synonymous with a stowage plan which has the same format but is drawn up to show the actual locations of all the consignments once they have been stowed in the ship.

cargo sharing reserving by the authorities of a country of the ocean carriage of its exports and imports to the ships of its own fleet and that of the countries with which it trades, usually in equal proportions, often allowing the ships of other countries a smaller share.

cargo superintendent person employed by a shipowner or shipping company to advise on the most efficient and safest distribution of cargo in the ship's holds, taking account of the various ports of discharge at which the ship will be calling and the nature of the goods.

cargo sweat condensation which occurs when a ship sails from a cool to a relatively warm climate. The temperature of the cargo rises at a slower rate than that of the ship's environment and when the surface of the cargo is colder than the dew point of the surrounding air, moisture condenses directly on to the cargo. Opinions differ as to whether cargo should be ventilated when meeting these climatic conditions, so as to avoid damage caused by cargo sweat.

cargo tank   ship's tank used for the carriage of cargo, as opposed to, for example, a ballast tank.

cargoworthiness   fitness of a ship to carry a particular cargo.

cargoworthy   said of a ship, being fit to carry a particular cargo.

carpenter   rating responsible for the woodwork on a ship.

carrier   party who enters into a contract of carriage with a shipper. The carrier may be the owner or charterer of a ship.

carryings   quantity of cargo carried over a period of time by a shipping line or by all the member lines of a liner conference. This quantity is a factor in determining the profitability of the service and the need, if any, to apply an increase to the freight rates.

cash against documents   term of sale whereby the buyer receives the commercial documents, including the bill of lading, which is the document of title, on paying the seller for the goods. This term is also used to qualify a contract of carriage in which the carrier releases the bill of lading to the shipper in exchange for the freight.

c.b.r.   *see* **commodity box rate.**

ceiling   timber placed on the floor of a ship's hold to protect it from damage.

cell   compartment in the hold of a containership into which a shipping container fits exactly. Also referred to as a **slot**.

cell guide   one of four uprights comprising a cell in a containership into which a container fits exactly. These uprights hold the container in position.

cellular containership   ship specially constructed to carry standard size shipping containers in cells, that is, in compartments into which the containers fit exactly.

cellular double bottom   space between the floor of a ship's holds and the bottom of the ship. Its purpose is to help prevent sea water entering the ship in the event of running aground. Made up of separate compartments, it is used for the carriage of fuel oil or fresh water or, if the ship is not carrying a cargo, for water ballast.

Cemenco   voyage charter-party used for shipments of cement, devised by the Chamber of Shipping of the United Kingdom.

C.E.N.S.A.   *see* **Council of European and Japanese National Shipowners' Associations.**

centistokes   measure of the viscosity of oils such as fuel oils. The greater the number of centistokes, the higher the viscosity of a grade of fuel.

centre-line bulkhead   vertical separation in a ship which runs lengthways along a ship, except underneath the hatchways. This type of bulkhead is constructed in order to provide the ship with additional longitudinal strength.

Centrocon   voyage charter-party used for shipments of grain from the River Plate.

certificate of seaworthiness   document issued by a surveyor after repairs have been effected certifying that the ship is seaworthy.

certificated officer   one of a number of officially qualified persons serving on a merchant ship. The number of certificated officers required on a ship may vary according to the country of registry, the ship's tonnage and the sort of trade (home trade, foreign-going) in which she is involved.

cesser clause   clause in a voyage charter-party which seeks to relieve the charterer of all responsibility under the contract once the cargo has been shipped. Often this clause incorporates a provision for the shipowner to have a lien on the cargo for freight, deadfreight and demurrage.

c. & f.   *see* **cost and freight.**

c.f.s.   *see* **container freight station.**

charter   (1)   the chartering or hiring of a ship. A ship which is hired out is said to be **on charter** and the time during which a ship is hired out is known as the **period of the charter**.

charter   (2)   short form for charter-party. *For definition, see* **charter-party**.

charter (to)   to hire a ship. This may be said of a shipowner, who hires or charters his ship out to a charterer, or of a charterer who hires or charters the ship from the shipowner.

charter by demise   the hiring or leasing of a ship for a period of time during which the shipowner provides only the ship while the charterer provides the crew together with all stores and bunkers and pays all the operating costs. This type of charter is favoured by persons or companies who wish to own a ship for investment purposes but who do not have the desire or expertise to operate the ship. Similarly, it is favoured by those who have a particular requirement for a ship and the expertise with which to operate one but without the wish or ability to purchase. Also known as a **bareboat charter** or **demise charter**.

charter by demise (to)   to hire or lease a ship for a period of time during which the shipowner provides only the ship while the charterer provides the crew together with all stores and bunkers and pays all the operating costs. Also known as **to demise charter** and **to bareboat charter**.

charter in (to)   to hire a ship from a shipowner. This expression is sometimes used more specifically to denote that the ship is being chartered for a specific voyage or purpose, supplementing a shipping company's fleet whose ships are fully committed or more profitably employed elsewhere.

charter out (to)   to hire a ship out to a charterer. This expression is sometimes used to denote, more specifically, the hiring out of a ship which is temporarily surplus to the requirements of a shipowner or shipping company.

charter party   *see* **charter-party** *below*.

charterable   said of a quantity of goods, sufficient to fill a ship taken on charter terms.

charterer   person or company who hires a ship from a shipowner for a period of time (*see* **time charterer**) or who reserves the entire cargo space of a ship for the carriage of goods from a port or ports of loading to a port or ports of discharge (*see* **voyage charterer**).
   in charterers' option   term in a charter-party which stipulates that the charterers have a choice in specific circumstances. For example, charterers may have the choice of discharge ports, one of which is to be declared to the shipowner by a certain point in the voyage.

charterer by demise   person or company who charters a ship for a period of time, provides crew, bunkers and stores and pays all operating costs. Also known as a **demise charterer** or **bareboat charterer**.

25

charterer's agent   ship's agent nominated by the voyage charterer in accordance with the charter-party. Although nominated by the charterer, the agent is paid by, and is responsible to, the shipowner. *See also* **ship's agent**.

charterer's bill of lading   bill of lading issued by a charterer and signed by him or his agent. Under certain circumstances, the charterer who signs his own bills of lading may be deemed to be the carrier, thus taking on all the responsibilities of a carrier.

chartering agent   shipowner who acts on behalf of a charterer in the negotiations leading to the chartering of a ship.

charter-party   document containing all the terms and conditions of the contract between a shipowner and a charterer, and signed by both parties or their agents, for the hire of a ship or the space in a ship. Most charter-parties are standard forms with printed clauses and spaces or boxes in which details relating to the individual charter, such as freight, laytime, demurrage, the ship's construction, speed and consumption, are inserted. The printed document may be varied and/or added to by agreement of the two parties. Sometimes spelled **charterparty** or **charter party**.

charter-party bill of lading   bill of lading issued for a shipment of cargo on a chartered ship when it is intended that the receiver be bound by the terms and conditions of the charter-party. A clause to this effect incorporating the date and place of signature of the charter-party appears on the bill of lading.

chassis   trailer on which a shipping container is secured when being moved by road vehicle or tractor.

chemicals tanker   ship designed to carry several grades of liquid cargo, particularly chemicals.

chopt.   in charterers' option. *See under* **charterer**.

c.i.f.   *see* **cost, insurance and freight**.

c.i.f.c.   cost, insurance, freight and commision.

c.i.f.f.o.   *see* **cost, insurance and freight, free out**.

C.I.M.   international convention on the carriage of goods by rail. It sets out the conditions of carriage for the international movement of goods by rail and the liabilities of the carrier.

c.i.p. *see* **calling-in-point.**

c.k.d. *see* **completely knocked down.**

claims adjuster employee of an insurance company whose job is to determine whether, or to what extent, claims presented by policy-holders are covered by the policies. The claims adjuster also has the task of recovering amounts paid out from carriers and other parties responsible.

class (1) one of a number of categories in the tariff of a shipping line or liner conference, each of which consists of a single freight rate and a group of commodities to which that rate applies. The classes are numbered for ease of identification and may include the suffix W or M denoting that freight is payable on the weight or measurement respectively (*see* **weight rated cargo** *and* **measurement rated cargo**).

class (2) category in a classification register denoting the type of ship and the classification society with which she is classed. Probably the best known class is 100A1 used by Lloyd's Register of Shipping and other classification societies. The assigning of a class depends on the ship being constructed and maintained in accordance with the classification society's rules.

classification certificate certificate issued by a classification society which states the class attributed to a ship.

classification register publication issued by a classification society which lists all the ships classed by that society and, in some cases, notably Lloyd's Register of Shipping, all other ships over a certain size. Against each ship is recorded such information as the place and date of build, the tonnages and capacities, dimensions, number of decks, holds and hatches and details of engines and boilers.

classification society organization whose main function is to carry out surveys of ships whilst being built and at regular intervals after construction, its purpose being to set and maintain standards of construction and upkeep for ships and their equipment. Each classification society has a set of rules governing the requirements for surveys and, for a ship to maintain her class, she must comply with these rules. In most countries, it is not obligatory for a shipowner to have his ship classed but there would be considerable difficulties in trading if the ship were not since it is often a condition of the ship's insurance and a requirement of most charterers and shippers. Classification societies also inspect and approve the construction of shipping containers. These organizations exist in most of the principal maritime countries.

27

classification survey survey carried out by a surveyor of a classification society, either a periodical survey or one required, for example, after a collision, to ensure that the ship meets the minimum standards for continued trading set by the classification society.

clause paramount clause in a bill of lading or charter-party which stipulates that the contract of carriage is governed by the Hague Rules or Hague-Visby Rules or the enactment of these rules of the country having jurisdiction over the contract.

claused bill of lading bill of lading containing one, or more than one, superimposed clause which may either specify a defect to the cargo or its packing, or may be any comment of the master regarding the carriage of the goods, for example, that the weight or contents of a consignment are unknown to him, or that goods shipped on deck are at the shipper's risk.

clean bill of lading bill of lading which contains no superimposed clauses specifying any defect to the cargo or its packing; it indicates that the cargo has been received by the ship in apparent good order and condition. Clean bills of lading are often required by banks who use them as collateral security against money advanced for the purchase of the goods described therein.

clean (petroleum) products refined products such as aviation spirit, motor spirit and kerosene. Also referred to as **white products**.

clean receipt receipt given by anyone receiving cargo into his care or possession bearing no clausing or notation indicating loss or damage, thus indicating that the goods were received in apparent good order and condition.

clean the holds (to) to sweep the holds of a ship and, if necessary, to wash them down after a cargo has been discharged so that they are clean in readiness for the next cargo. It is often a requirement of time charter-parties that the holds of the ship be clean or clean-swept on delivery to the time charterer at the beginning of the period of the charter and, similarly, on redelivery to the shipowner at the end of the charter.

clear days period of time excluding the first and last days.

clearance outwards permission granted by the Customs authorities at a port for a ship to proceed to sea. This is granted after production by the master or agent of the ship's safety certificates and outward cargo manifest.

clip-on unit generator which can be attached to a refrigerated container to provide auxiliary power.

close (to)   to complete loading. Generally only said of a liner ship.

closed conference   liner conference in which the member lines vote on the admission of a new line. The purpose of this is to restrict the number of ships in a particular trade. *For definition of* liner conference, *see* **conference**.

closed shelter-deck ship *or* **closed shelter-decker**   ship, constructed as a shelter-decker, whose tonnage opening has been sealed, effectively converting her to a two deck ship similar to a tween decker. *See also* **shelter-deck ship** *and* **tonnage opening**.

closing date   final date for delivering cargo to a liner ship.

closure of navigation   closure to shipping of an area or waterway, often because of severe ice conditions during winter.

C.M.R.   international convention on the carriage of goods by road. It sets out the conditions of carriage for the international movement of goods by road and the liabilities of the carrier.

coaming   steel surround to a hatchway which rises vertically from the deck of a ship. Its functions are to prevent water from entering the hold and to lessen the risk of any person who may be working on the deck falling through the open hatchway. Also referred to as a **hatch coaming**.

Coastcon   voyage charter-party used for shipments of coal, devised by the Chamber of Shipping of the United Kingdom. The full name of this charter-party is the Chamber of Shipping Coasting Coal Charter-party.

coaster   ship which carries cargoes between ports on the same coast or ports of the same country. This term is also used occasionally to refer to short sea traders, that is, ships which perform short international voyages.

Coasthire   time charter-party, the full name of which is the Chamber of Shipping Coasting and Short Sea Daily Hire Charter Party.

coasting broker   shipbroker who specializes in the negotiation of charters for coastwise or short sea voyages.

coastwise   along, or around, a coast. Said of movements of cargo carried in this way, generally by relatively small ships.

coil carrier   shipping container, resembling a flatrack, which has a depression

29

known as a well in which steel coils rest to prevent them from moving when in transit.

collapsible flatrack shipping container, consisting of a flat bed and four corner posts, designed to carry cargoes of awkward size. When these flatracks are empty, the ends are collapsed and several flatracks may then be interlocked in a stack which has the same dimensions as a single standard container enabling them to be transported in the same way.

collapsible mast ship's mast which is capable of being folded down to enable the ship to pass under a bridge or series of bridges.

collier ship designed to be used for the carriage of coal, with very wide hatchways to provide for fast loading and discharging.

Combiconbill combined transport bill of lading adopted by the Baltic and International Maritime Conference (B.I.M.C.O.). *For definition, see* **combined transport bill of lading** *below*.

Combidoc combined transport document issued by the Baltic and International Maritime Conference (B.I.M.C.O.). *For definition, see* **combined transport bill of lading** *below*.

combinable cranes two ship's cranes which can be employed together so as to make use of their combined lifting capacity when handling lifts in excess of their individual capacities.

combination carrier ship whose construction allows the carriage of either bulk cargoes, such as ore, or cargoes of oil. The purpose is to reduce the amount of time a ship would spend in ballast, that is, without a cargo, if she were only capable of carrying one type of cargo. Additionally, such ships are able to select the commodity which provides the best return. Examples of combination carriers are ore/oil carriers and ore/bulk/oil carriers.

combined transport bill of lading *or* **combined transport document** document evidencing a contract between a shipper and a shipping line for the carriage of goods on a voyage involving at least two legs. Normally, the issuer of this document is responsible for the goods from the time they are received into his care until the time they are delivered at destination.

come forward (1) said of a ship, to have an estimated date or time of arrival, readiness or completion of loading or discharging, as the case may be, which is earlier than previously advised or expected.

30

come forward (2) said of cargo, to arrive at the ship for loading. This term is usually qualified by the date or method of delivery to the ship.

commodity box rate freight rate per shipping container for a particular commodity.

common berth *or* **common user berth** berth whose use is not restricted to the ships of any one shipping line or company.

common carrier person or company advertising a service involving the carriage of goods to and from ports on a particular route. A common carrier is required by law to accept all cargoes offered, except dangerous ones, and to make a reasonable charge for their carriage.

common short form bill of lading type of bill of lading which may be used by any shipping line since neither the name of the line nor its conditions of carriage are printed on it: the name is typed on and a printed clause states that the full terms and conditions are available on request.

completely knocked down said of cargo, normally of cars, shipped in pieces and cased, to be assembled at destination.

compulsory pilotage legal obligation for a ship to use the services of a pilot in a particular place. In some places, pilotage is only compulsory for ships over a certain size or for masters who have not navigated a particular waterway a minimum number of times.

Conbill bill of lading approved by the Baltic and International Maritime Conference (B.I.M.C.O.) for use when no charter-party is signed.

condensation turning of water vapour into liquid which occurs when a ship sails from a cool to a relatively warm climate (*see* **cargo sweat**) or vice versa (*see* **ship's sweat**). Often, the expert use of ventilation is required to prevent condensation which can cause serious damage to cargoes.

conference two or more shipping lines operating a service in common between designated geographical areas. The lines agree a set of freight rates and any special rates for shippers and each line charges the same as the others. The ships used are of types suitable for the trade. Unlike tramp shipping where freight rates are a function of daily supply and demand, conference rates are relatively stable: base rates are altered by means of a general rate increase which in many cases is once a year. Lines in a conference are governed by the rules of membership which may include rights to load or discharge at certain ports and pooling of cargo. Also referred to as a **freight conference** or a **shipping conference** or a **liner conference**.

conference secretariat   administrative office of a liner conference which acts as co-ordinator for its member lines. Its functions include publishing a freight tariff and periodic amendments to it, keeping shippers informed of proposed changes to the level of surcharges and receiving requests from shippers for special freight rates and conveying the responses and offers of the lines.

conference terms   qualification to a freight which signifies that it is subject to the standard terms and conditions of the particular liner conference. These are normally set out in the conference's tariff.

Congenbill   bill of lading intended to be used with charter-parties. One of the clauses in this bill of lading states that it incorporates all the terms of the charter-party.

congestion   accumulation of ships at a port to the extent that ships arriving to load or discharge are obliged to wait for a vacant berth. There are various reasons for congestion, such as strikes, severe weather or a seasonally high number of cargoes. When liner ships suffer prolonged delays, their operators very often charge shippers a congestion surcharge.

congestion surcharge   extra charge applied by shipping lines and liner conferences to reflect the cost of delay to their ships at a particular port caused by congestion.

Conlinebill   liner bill of lading published by the Baltic and International Maritime Conference (B.I.M.C.O.). *See* **liner bill of lading**.

Conlinebooking   liner booking note published by the Baltic and International Maritime Conference (B.I.M.C.O.). *See* **booking note**.

consecutive voyages   successive voyages of a ship on charter to one party. The charter-party may stipulate the number of voyages or the total quantity of cargo to be carried or the total period during which the shipowner performs the maximum number of voyages.

consign (to)   to place goods in the care of a carrier for delivery to a person known as the consignee.

consignee   person to whom goods are to be delivered by the carrier at the place of destination.

consignment   (1) goods which are placed in the care of a carrier for delivery to a person known as the consignee.

consignment   (2) act of placing goods in the care of a carrier for delivery to a person known as the consignee.

consignment note   document, prepared by the shipper, which contains details of the consignment to be carried to the port of loading. It is signed by the inland carrier as proof of receipt into his care.

consignor   person who places goods in the care of a carrier for delivery to a person known as the consignee.

consolidation   the grouping together of several compatible consignments into a full container load. Also referred to as **groupage**.

consortium   group of shipping lines, normally members of a liner conference, who pool their ships and other resources to provide a combined service in a particular trade.

constants   combined weight of a ship's stores and spares. This weight, normally expressed in tons or tonnes, is taken into consideration when calculating the maximum quantity of cargo, bunkers and fresh water which the ship can lift.

constructive total loss   loss or damage to goods or to a ship which is such that the cost of repair or recovery would exceed their value when repaired or recovered.

consulage   fee paid to a consul for the protection of goods.

consumption (of bunkers)   quantity of fuel oil and diesel oil consumed each day by a ship's engines. This varies according to whether the ship is at sea or in port.

contact inhibitor   substance which is designed to inhibit corrosion to certain metals when submitted to varying climatic conditions. It is usually contained in the paper used to wrap these products for shipment.

container   box, of which there are several standard sizes, designed to enable goods to be sent from door to door without the contents being handled. To this end, special road and rail vehicles and special ships were designed for their carriage. The general purpose container carries a wide range of products and there are many other types of container for specific purposes, for example, tank containers designed to carry liquids, refrigerated containers which carry temperature controlled goods including dairy products, side door, end door and open top containers. The container is widely referred to as a **box**.

container berth   place alongside a quay where containerships load and discharge, normally equipped with cranes, tractors and trailers and straddle carriers for moving the containers to and from stacking areas.

container capacity   total number of shipping containers, generally expressed as a number of t.e.u.'s (twenty foot equivalent units), which may be accommodated on board a ship.

container freight station   place where consignments are grouped together and packed into a shipping container or where such consignments are unpacked.

container leasing   hiring of a shipping container for a voyage or period of time, normally based on a daily hire rate.

container port   port whose only, or principal, traffic is in shipping containers. Its berths are equipped with container cranes and there are large areas for stacking the containers prior to loading on to the ship or after discharging.

container terminal   part of a port where containers are loaded on to, and discharged from, containerships.

container yard   place to which full container loads are delivered by the shipper to the ocean carrier and to which empty containers are returned.

containerable *or* **containerizable**   said of cargo which is capable of being loaded into a shipping container.

containerization   the employment by shipping lines of containerships and the discontinuing of the use of conventional ships.

containerize (to)   (1) to put cargo into a shipping container.

containerize (to)   (2) as a shipping line or a number of shipping lines, to employ only containerships for a particular route, service or trade and discontinue the use of conventional ships.

containerized   (1) said of cargo which has been put into a shipping container.

containerized (2) said of a particular route, service or trade which is served only by containerships, the use of conventional ships having been discontinued.

containership ship specially designed to carry shipping containers. She has cells into which the containers are lowered and where they are held in place by uprights called cell guides. Containers are frequently carried on deck where they require to be lashed and secured.

contamination (of cargo) tainting of cargo by virtue of its being stowed in close proximity to a product with a strong smell or in a compartment which previously contained such a product and which has not been cleaned. Tea is an example of a commodity which can be contaminated in this way.

contract of affreightment contract for the hire of a ship. Often defined also as a contract for a series of voyages involving bulk cargoes.

contractor person or company having a loyalty contract with a liner conference and entitled, subject to having complied with the terms of the contract, to a contractor's rebate.

contributory value value of property at the end of a voyage in which there has been a general average loss. This forms the basis of the contribution by each of the parties to the voyage to make good the loss.

conventional relating to dry cargo lifted on and off ships one piece, or bundle, at a time by means of cranes or derricks, but not shipped on trailers or in shipping containers. Such goods may be described as **conventional cargo**; the ships which carry them are sometimes referred to as **conventional ships** which, if operated on a regular basis between advertised ports, provide a **conventional service**. Also referred to as **breakbulk**.

convoy group of ships escorted along a stretch of water. For instance, on a canal which is not wide enough for ships sailing in opposite directions to pass each other, the most efficient solution is for ships to transit in convoy, first in one direction, then the other.

c.o.p. *see* **custom of the port**.

copy bill of lading reproduction of a bill of lading intended to be used for administrative purposes only and not for taking delivery of the goods or for transferring title to them.

CORE7 voyage charter-party used widely for shipments of iron ore.

corner casting *or* **corner fitting**   fitting located at each of the corners of a shipping container by means of which the container is handled and lifted.

corresponding draught   depth to which a ship is immersed in water corresponding to a particular deadweight, that is, when carrying a particular quantity of cargo, fuel, fresh water and stores.

cost and freight   sales term denoting that the seller is responsible for arranging and paying for the carriage of the goods to the agreed port of discharge. Risk of loss or damage generally passes to the buyer when the goods pass ship's rail at the port of loading.

cost insurance and freight   sales term denoting that the seller is responsible for arranging and paying for the carriage of the goods to the agreed port of discharge and for the insurance of the goods covering the period of carriage involved in the contract of sale. The risk of loss or damage generally passes to the buyer when the goods pass ship's rail at the port of loading.

cost insurance and freight free out *or* **cost insurance and freight ship's hold**   identical to cost insurance and freight above except that the cost and responsibility of discharging the ship are borne by the buyer. Since the seller has no control over the discharging of the cargo, the contract of sale may stipulate the number of hours or days allowed to the buyer to discharge and a rate of demurrage if this period is exceeded. Alternatively, if the carriage is performed by a ship chartered by the seller, the terms of the charter-party may be imposed on the buyer.

Council of European and Japanese National Shipowners' Associations   organization, consisting of shipowners from a number of countries, whose purpose is to represent the views of its members in all matters related to shipping with, for example, governments and shippers' bodies.

count (as laytime) (to)   to be included in the calculation of laytime in a voyage charter. Whether a period, such as during a week-end or a strike, counts as laytime is subject to the agreement of shipowner and charterer save that, once all the time allowed has been used, the remaining period until completion of loading or discharging, as the case may be, counts without exception. A typical voyage charter-party clause might stipulate that "time between 1700 hours Friday and 0800 hours Monday not to count, even if used".

counter-offer *or* **counter**   response to an offer which in some way varies the terms or conditions of that offer. By virtue of a party making a counter-offer, the

36

offer itself is no longer binding. Offer and counter-offer form the basis of the negotiations involved in chartering ships.

counter-offer (to) *or* **counter (to)**   to respond to an offer varying in some way the terms or conditions of that offer. *See also* **counter-offer** *above*.

c.o.w.   *see* **crude oil washing**.

c/p   *see* **charter-party**.

c.p.d.   charterer pays dues.

c.p.p.   *see* **clean petroleum products**.

cr.   (1) crane.

cr.   (2) credit.

cranage   the use of a crane. Sometimes used to define the charges paid for the use of a crane.

crane   machine for lifting and moving heavy weights. Cranes may be mobile (on wheels or tracks), floating or fixed to the shore or to the deck of a ship.

crosstrade (to)   to trade a ship wherever suitable cargoes are available, rather than carrying cargoes to and from the country where the ship is registered.

crude oil washing   system of cleaning the tanks of a tanker by washing them with the cargo of crude oil while it is being discharged.

c.s.d.   *see* **closed shelter deck ship**.

cst.   *see* **centistokes**.

c.t.   *see* **conference terms**.

c.t.l.   *see* **constructive total loss**.

cu. ft.   cubic feet.

currency adjustment factor   surcharge applied to freight rates by shipping lines and liner conferences. The purpose of the currency adjustment factor (c.a.f.) is embodied in the E.S.C. (European Shippers' Councils)/C.E.N.S.A.

(Council of European and Japanese National Shipowners' Associations) Code. It is to ensure that the revenue of the shipping lines is unaffected by movements in the currencies in which transactions are carried out by the lines in relation to the tariff currency. The Code provides formulae, adopted by many conferences, for calculating the c.a.f. and, since the values of currencies can move upwards as well as downwards, the c.a.f., which is normally expressed as a percentage of the freight, may be negative as well as positive. Thus a tariff rate of $100 becomes $108 when subject to a +8 per cent c.a.f. and $95 when the c.a.f. is −5 per cent.

currency and bunker adjustment factor   surcharge applied by some shipping lines and liner conferences which consists of a currency adjustment factor and a bunker adjustment factor combined. This surcharge is normally expressed as a percentage of the freight rate. *See also* **currency adjustment factor** *and* **bunker surcharge**.

custom of the port   established practice at a port which becomes part of a contract of carriage unless otherwise provided for in the contract. Frequent examples are the daily rate of loading and discharging, and the point where a carrier's responsibility ends in a liner terms contract.

customary assistance   assistance given by the master and crew to a time charterer which would normally be given to the shipowner were he operating the ship himself. Examples of customary assistance are the cleaning of the ship's holds when in ballast, the opening and closing of hatches and the lashing and unlashing of shipping containers carried on deck.

Customs agent   person whose business is to clear goods through Customs on behalf of cargo interests.

Customs clearance   permission by Customs authorities for goods to be brought into or out of a country.

Customs manifest   copy of the ship's manifest which is submitted to the Customs authorities. In some countries, a special form or lay-out is required. *See also* **manifest**.

c.y.   *see* **container yard**.

D

daily running cost   cost per day of operating a ship. It includes wages, stores, provisions, repairs, insurance and protection and indemnity club calls, but generally excludes voyage expenses such as bunkers, cargo handling costs and agency fees. Also excluded generally is any allowance for depreciation or replacement of the ship.

damages for detention   sum of money payable to the shipowner by the voyage charterer, or anyone who becomes a party to the terms of the charter, for failing to load and/or discharge cargo within the time allowed in the charter-party. It is payable for each day or part thereafter until completion of loading or discharging, as the case may be. Unlike demurrage, the amount is not agreed in advance, but is normally set by the Court either at the same rate as demurrage if such a rate has been incorporated into the charter-party, or based on the daily running cost of the ship plus any profit which the shipowner might reasonably have expected. These damages apply when the charter-party contains no provision for demurrage or when the agreed period of demurrage is exceeded.

dangerous goods   cargo which is potentially hazardous such as inflammable or toxic goods. Such cargo must be notified by the shipper to the shipping company as being dangerous and is usually carried on deck.

d.b.b.   deals, battens and boards—unit of measure of timber.

deadfreight   amount of money payable by a shipper or charterer to a ship-owner or shipping line for failing to load the quantity of cargo stipulated in the contract of carriage. Deadfreight is normally payable at the full freight rate but may be reduced by the loading and/or discharging expenses if these were included in the freight.

deadweight *or* **deadweight all told**   difference between a ship's loaded and light displacements, consisting of the total weight of cargo, fuel, fresh water, stores and crew which a ship can carry when immersed to a particular load line, normally her summer load line. The deadweight is expressed in tons or tonnes. Also referred to as **total deadweight**.

deadweight cargo   cargo one tonne of which measures one cubic metre or less. Freight on deadweight cargo is generally payable on the weight, that is, per tonne or per ton. Also referred to as **weight cargo.**

deadweight cargo capacity *or* **deadweight carrying capacity**   weight of

39

cargo which a ship is able to carry when immersed to the appropriate load line, expressed in tonnes or tons.

deadweight scale   table which shows in columns a set of draughts with a ship's corresponding deadweight tonnages when she is lying in salt water and fresh water.

deballast (to)   to remove the ballast from a ship. In the case of water ballast, this entails pumping it overboard.

deck   covering of all or part of the hull of a ship into which hatchways are cut to give access to the holds.

deck cargo   cargo carried on, and secured to, the open deck of a ship. Cargoes traditionally carried on deck include dangerous goods, timber and goods which are too large for the hatchways. Deck cargoes are carried at the risk of the charterer, shipper or bill of lading holder, as the case may be.

deck line   line, 12 inches or 300 millimetres long, painted amidships on both sides of a ship and parallel to the load lines. This line is located at the point where the uppermost continuous deck, known as the freeboard deck, meets the side of the ship. The distances between the deck line and each of the load lines represent the ship's minimum freeboards allowable in the various load line zones.

deck option   option required from a shipper by a shipowner or shipping line to carry goods on deck in the event that stowage under deck is not feasible, for example, when goods are likely to be too large for the hatchways or when the holds of a ship are expected to be full of cargo but the ship still has some deadweight capacity.

declare general average (to)   to declare to all parties involved in a voyage that an intentional act or sacrifice has been carried out in order to protect the voyage from a real peril. This declaration is made by the shipowner who appoints a general average adjuster to determine each party's contribution to the loss.

deep sea (trade)   long distance international maritime trade.

deep tank   tank situated between the holds of a ship, primarily used for water ballast but capable of carrying water or fuel.

deferred rebate   discount on the freight, offered by a liner conference to a shipper, which is payable at some agreed time, normally several months, after the date of shipment, provided that the shipper does not ship any cargo during this period with a non-conference line to any destination served by the conference.

deliver (to) (cargo)   as carrier, to convey goods to the receiver or bill of lading holder at the place of destination in the contract of carriage.

deliver (to) (a ship)   as shipowner, to place a time chartered ship at the disposal of the charterer at the beginning of the period of the charter, at the place and time agreed. *See also* **delivery (of a ship)** *below*.

delivered   sales term denoting that the seller is responsible for arranging and paying for the carriage of the goods to the place agreed in the contract. The seller bears the risk of loss or damage to the goods until they are delivered to that place. The contract should specify whether it is the buyer's or seller's responsibility to arrange Customs clearance and pay any import duty. Also referred to as **free delivered** and **franco domicile**.

delivery (of cargo)   the conveying of goods by a carrier to the receiver or bill of lading holder at the place of destination in the contract of carriage.

delivery (of a ship)   placing of a time chartered ship by the shipowner at the disposal of the charterer at the beginning of the period of the charter, at the time and place agreed. The place of delivery is often a location, such as a pilot station, where it is relatively easy to verify the time of arrival and hence the time when the charter commences. Normally, an on hire survey is carried out as soon as practicable in order to determine the condition of the ship and the quantity of bunkers on board at the time of delivery.

delivery certificate   document, signed by or on behalf of the shipowner and the charterer, certifying the time, date and place of delivery of the ship, that is, the placing of the ship at the disposal of the time charterer at the beginning of the period of the charter. The certificate also states the quantity of bunkers on board at the time of delivery and any notations by the charterer concerning the failure of the ship to comply in any respect with the terms of the charter-party.

delivery order   document issued by a liner company's agent authorizing the party named in it to take delivery of specific cargo from a ship. It is normally issued in exchange for an original bill of lading.

demise charter   (1) the hiring or leasing of a ship for a period of time during which the shipowner provides only the ship while the charterer provides the crew together with all stores and bunkers and pays all the operating costs. This type of charter is favoured by persons or companies who wish to own a ship for investment purposes but who do not have the desire or expertise to operate the ship. Similarly, it is favoured by persons or companies who have a particular requirement for a ship and the expertise with which to operate one but without the wish or ability to purchase. A ship hired out in this way is said to be **on demise charter**. Also referred to as a **bareboat charter** or a **charter by demise**.

demise charter (2) short form for demise charter-party. *For definition, see* **demise charter-party** *below*.

demise charter (to) to hire or lease a ship for a period of time during which the shipowner provides only the ship while the charterer provides the crew together with all stores and bunkers and pays all the operating costs. Also known known as **to charter by demise** and **to bareboat charter**.

demise charterer person or company who charters a ship for a period of time, provides crew, bunkers and stores and pays all operating costs. Also known as a **charterer by demise** or **bareboat charterer**.

demise charter-party document containing the contract between the owner of a ship and the demise charterer, and signed by both, in which are all the terms and conditions such as the period of the charter, the rate of hire, the trading limits and all the rights and responsibilities of the two parties. Also referred to as a **bareboat charter-party**.

demise clause clause in a bill of lading stipulating that the contract of carriage is between the shipper or bill of lading holder and the shipowner. Bills of lading issued by charterers of a ship on behalf of the owner and master often contain this clause. It should be noted that this clause is inconsistent with the laws of certain countries and may therefore be invalid in those countries.

demurrage (1) amount of money paid to the shipowner by the charterer, shipper or receiver, as the case may be, for failing to complete loading and/or discharging within the time allowed in the voyage charter-party. The rate of demurrage, normally an amount per day or part of a day, is agreed in the charter-party. Some charters specify that, after a certain period of demurrage, either additional demurrage or damages for detention become payable. When demurrage becomes payable, it is said of a ship that she is **on demurrage**. Once a ship is on demurrage, no deductions are made for excepted periods, such as weekends, in the calculation of the demurrage charges; hence it is said **once on demurrage, always on demurrage**.

demurrage (2) scheduled charge payable by a shipper or receiver to a shipping line for detaining equipment at a container yard beyond the time allowed.

depth of water factor at a port or place which may determine the type or maximum size of ship capable of reaching there and the maximum cargo which can be carried to or from it.

der. *see* **derrick.**

deratting extermination of rats carried out on board a ship for which a certificate is issued by the health authorities in a port.

deratting certificate document issued by the health authorities in a port which certifies that any rats on board a ship have been exterminated.

deratting exemption certificate document issued by the health authorities in a port which certifies that their inspector has found a ship to be free of rats.

derrick lifting equipment on board a ship consisting of a post attached to the deck and an inclined spar which swings between the quay and the hatchway. With the help of winches, the derrick is used primarily for loading and discharging cargo but is also used for stores.

despatch speed. Under English common law, it is implied in contracts of carriage that the shipowner must perform the voyage with reasonable despatch.

despatch (money) amount of money the rate of which is agreed in advance, payable by the shipowner to the charterer, shipper or receiver, as the case may be, for loading and/or discharging in less than the time allowed; normally, despatch money, if a provision for it has been made, is at the same rate as, or half the rate of, the rate of demurrage agreed in the charter-party.

destuff (to) to unload a shipping container.

Det Norske Veritas Norwegian ship classification society. *For the functions of a ship classification society, see* **classification society**.

detention charge charge payable by a shipper or receiver to a shipping line for detaining equipment beyond the time allowed.

dets. details. *For definition, see* **subject details**.

43

deviation   departure by a ship from the agreed route or normal trade route.

deviation clause   clause in a bill of lading or charter-party allowing the shipping line or shipowner to deviate from the agreed route or normal trade route. This clause varies from contract to contract and may permit the ship to call at unscheduled ports for whatever reason, or to deviate to save life or property.

dew point   temperature at which condensation first occurs and moisture is formed. If the temperature of the outside air falls below that within a confined space such as the hold of a ship or a shipping container, moisture forms on the interior steelwork of the ship or container. If, on the other hand, the temperature of the outside air rises above that of the interior of the ship or container, moisture forms directly on the cargo. It is necessary, in certain circumstances, to ventilate a ship's hold in order to change the dew point temperature, thus avoiding condensation.

diesel oil   oil used to power a ship's auxiliary equipment and, when manœuvring in confined spaces, the main engines.

direct continuation   extension to the period of a time charter, available in some charter-parties as an option to the charterer.

direct discharge   the removal of goods from a ship directly on to road vehicles or railway wagons, that is, without being put on to the quay. When instructed to deliver cargo in this way, shipping lines often insert a clause in the bill of lading to the effect that this will be carried out provided that sufficient wagons or vehicles are available to ensure that there is no delay in the discharging of the ship.

direct transhipment   transfer of cargo from one ship to another in one operation, thus avoiding the need to put the cargo to quay with consequent extra cost and handling. Cargoes are frequently transhipped direct from barge or short sea ship on to ocean ships.

dirty bill of lading   bill of lading containing one, or more than one, superimposed clause specifying a defect to the cargo or packing, noted at the time the goods are received by the ship. Such a bill of lading is also referred to as foul or unclean.

dirty (petroleum) products   crude oils, such as heavy fuel oils. Also referred to as **black products**.

disbursements   sums paid out by a ship's agent at a port and recovered from the shipowner by means of a disbursements account. Typical expenses include port charges, pilotage, towage and the agent's fee.

disbursements account   account rendered by a ship's agent at a port to the shipowner for all sums paid out in respect of the ship's call at the port such as pilotage, towage, port charges, any cash advance to the master, supply of provisions and stores and the agency fee. The account is supported by receipts known as vouchers.

discharge (to)   to remove goods from a ship.

dispatch   alternative spelling for despatch. *For definition, see* **despatch (money)** *and* **despatch** *above.*

dispensation   agreement, given by a liner conference to a shipper who has a loyalty contract, allowing the shipper to use a non-conference shipping line for a particular consignment. This may be given, for example, when the conference lines are unable to accommodate the consignment because of lack of space on board their ships or because they do not have a sailing at the right time to comply with the delivery requirements of the consignee.

displacement *or* **displacement tonnage**   weight of water displaced by a ship.

displacement scale   table which shows in columns a set of draughts with a ship's corresponding displacement tonnages when she is lying in salt water and fresh water.

disponent owner   person or company who controls the commercial operation of a ship, responsible for deciding the ports of call and the cargoes to be carried. Very often, the disponent owner is a shipping line which time charters a ship and issues its own liner bills of lading.

dly.   *see* **delivery**.

D.N.V.   Det Norske Veritas—Norwegian ship classification society. *For the functions of a ship classification society, see* **classification society**.

d.o.   *see* **diesel oil**.

dock   enclosed basin surrounded by quays used for loading and discharging ships.

dock dues   charge levied against a shipowner or ship operator by a port authority for the use of a dock.

docker   worker who loads and discharges ships.

dolphin   island mooring generally constructed of wooden piles or cement blocks.

donkey-engine   ship's auxiliary engine.

donkeyman   engine-room petty officer whose duties include being responsible for the maintenance of the ship's auxiliary engines.

door   watertight barrier which seals an opening in a roll-on roll-off ship through which rolling cargo is wheeled or driven along a ramp into or out of the ship. Doors are located either forward (bow doors), aft (stern doors) or at the sides (side doors) and are frequently made up of the ramps themselves which are operated hydraulically.

door to door   said of a service or freight rate provided by a container shipping line whereby goods are loaded into a shipping container at the shipper's premises and not unloaded until they arrive at the consignee's premises. Also referred to as **house to house**.

d.o.p.   *see* **dropping outward pilot**.

double bottom (tank)   space between the floor of a ship's holds and the bottom of the ship. Its purpose is to help prevent sea water entering the ship in the event of running aground. It is used for the carriage of fuel oil or fresh water or, if the ship is not carrying a cargo, for water ballast.

double-rigged   said of a hatchway which is served by two derricks.

down by the head   said of a ship whose draught forward is slightly deeper than her draught aft. This often makes the handling of a ship difficult at sea. Also referred to as **trimmed by the head**.

down by the stern   said of a ship whose draught aft is slightly deeper than her draught forward. Also referred to as **trimmed by the stern**.

down to her marks   said of a ship whose hull is immersed to the appropriate load line and which cannot therefore load any further cargo.

downtime   period during which equipment, such as a crane, is undergoing repairs or maintenance and cannot therefore be used.

d.p.p.   *see* **dirty petroleum products.**

draft   widely used alternative spelling of draught. *For definition, see* **draught** *below.*

draught   (1) depth to which a ship is immersed in the water; this depth varies according to the design of the ship and will be greater or lesser depending not only on the weight of the ship and everything on board, such as cargo, ballast, fuel and spares, but also on the density of the water in which the ship is lying.

draught   (2) widely used to designate the depth of water available at a port or place.

draught limitation   maximum depth of water to which the hull of a ship may be immersed at a certain port or place. Normally expressed in feet or metres, this figure is used in conjunction with the ship's deadweight scale to determine the quantity in tonnes of cargo, known as the lift, which the ship can carry.

draught marks   scale marked on a ship's stem and stern enabling her draught to be determined.

draught survey   survey undertaken at the discharge port to determine the quantity of cargo on board a ship. The survey is in two parts: before and after discharge. Prior to discharge, the surveyor ascertains the draughts forward and aft and, taking into consideration the density of the water in which the ship is lying and any hogging or sagging, calculates the ship's displacement tonnage. He then sounds the ship's tanks to determine the quantity of fuel, fresh water and ballast on board. After discharge he repeats the procedure and arrives at a new displacement tonnage. After making allowances for any fuel and fresh water used or taken on board during discharge as well as any ballast pumped aboard, he calculates the quantity of cargo. This is sometimes used as the basis on which payment is made for bulk cargoes.

draw (to)   to have a draught of (a certain number of feet or metres). For example, it may be said that a particular ship draws four metres when immersed to her summer load line.

drawback   repayment, when goods are re-exported, of duty previously paid on imported goods.

dredge (to)   to remove mud or sand from the sea bed or river bed. This is often done at or near a port to increase the depth of water or to restore it to its former depth.

drop back (to)   said of a ship, to have an estimated date or time of arrival, readiness or completion of loading or discharging, as the case may be, which is later than previously advised or expected. Also referred to as **to go back**.

dropping outward pilot   frequently used provision in a time charter to determine the time and place of redelivery of a ship to the owner by the charterer. The hire charge ceases at the moment the pilot disembarks.

dry cargo   said of any commodity which is not a liquid.

dry cargo container   shipping container which is designed for the carriage of goods other than liquids. Also referred to as a **dry freight container**.

dry dock   enclosed basin from which all the water is pumped to enable ships to be surveyed and repaired while out of the water. Ships offered for sale are normally inspected in a dry dock by prospective purchasers. Also referred to as a **graving dock**.

dry freight container   *see* **dry cargo container** *above.*

dry weight   actual weight of a bulk cargo less an allowance for moisture content.

dry-dock (to)   to put a ship into a dry dock, that is, an enclosed basin where she can be inspected or repaired while out of the water.

d.t.   *see* **deep tank**.

dual rate contract   system whereby a liner conference applies the same conditions of carriage to all shipments but whose tariff contains two sets of rates: one level for shippers who undertake to ship all, or an agreed amount, of their cargo on conference line ships, and a higher level for all other shippers.

duct keel   tunnel which accommodates pipelines and which runs longitudinally along the centre line of a ship under the inner plating.

dumb barge   barge which does not possess its own motive power.

dunnage   materials of various types, often timber or matting, placed among the cargo for separation, and hence protection from damage, for ventilation and, in the case of certain cargoes, to provide a space in which the forks of a fork-lift truck may be inserted.

dunnage (to)   to place dunnage material among a cargo. *See also* **dunnage** *above.*

d.w.a.t.   *see* **deadweight all told.**

d.w.c.c.   *see* **deadweight cargo capacity** *or* **deadweight carrying capacity** *above.*

d.w.t.   *see* **deadweight.**

d½d.   demurrage half despatch. This term, often found in voyage charter negotiations, signifies that despatch money is to be paid at half the daily rate of demurrage. The rate of demurrage precedes this term in the offer or counter-offer, as the case may be. For example, an offer by telex might read USD 5,000 d½d. which signifies that demurrage would be at the rate of U.S. Dollars 5,000 per day and despatch money at U.S. Dollars 2,500 per day.

E

earn despatch (to)   to be entitled to despatch money at the rate agreed in the charter-party by loading and/or discharging the cargo in less than the time allowed.

earn freight (to)   as a carrier, to fulfil sufficient of a contract of carriage for freight to be payable by the shipper. The point at which freight is earned is the subject of agreement between the two parties.

economical speed   speed of a ship which is lower than its normal speed and which may provide an overall saving comparing the reduction in fuel costs with the greater running cost arising from an increase in the duration of the voyage.

e.d.h.   *see* **efficient deck hand.**

efficient deck hand   seaman who is qualified by examination but who lacks the length of service at sea necessary to be an able seaman.

e.i.u. *see* **even if used**.

elevator   equipment used to discharge some bulk cargoes such as grain which is removed from the hold by a continuous line of buckets or by suction and carried on a conveyor belt to store.

endorse a bill of lading (to)   to sign over a bill of lading to another, thus transferring title to the goods described in the bill of lading to that party.

enter a ship (to)   to obtain insurance from a protection and indemnity club for a ship.

enter a ship in(wards) (to)   to report a ship's arrival to the Customs authorities at a port, providing particulars of the ship, its crew and cargo and details of the previous and subsequent voyages. This task is carried out by the master of the ship or his agent.

enter a ship out(wards) (to)   to seek the permission of the Customs authorities at a port for a ship to sail. This task is performed by the master or agent who provides safety certificates to show that the ship is safe to proceed to sea and a manifest of the cargo loaded.

entrepot   place where goods are imported and subsequently re-exported.

entry (in a tariff)   category in the tariff of a shipping line or liner conference representing a particular commodity or group of commodities for which there is a corresponding freight rate.

equipment handover charge   charge made by a shipping line for the loan of its equipment, such as containers or trailers, to a shipper or receiver who provides his own inland haulage. Also referred to as a **transfer charge**.

e.t.a.   estimated time of arrival.

e.t.c.   estimated time of completion.

e.t.d.   estimated time of departure.

e.t.r.   estimated time of readiness.

e.t.s.   estimated time of sailing.

even if used   term used in a voyage charter-party which provides that time used to load or discharge, as the case may be, during excepted periods is not deducted from time allowed. A charter-party might stipulate that time does not count from 1700 hours Friday to 0800 hours Monday, even if used. In this case, even if the charterer chooses to load or discharge in between these hours, the time spent working would not count as laytime.

even keel said of a ship whose draught forward is the same as her draught aft.

ex (1) formerly. When used immediately before the name of a ship, this means the former name of that ship. This information is useful in the case of a ship whose name has changed recently, as it enables a broker or prospective charterer to look her up under her former name in a classification register in order to ascertain details of her size and construction.

ex (2) from. This term is used with a location, for example, ex works, ex quay or ex ship, to identify the point where responsibility passes from one party to another.

ex quay sales term denoting that the seller is responsible for arranging and paying for the carriage of the goods to the agreed port of destination and for making them available on the quay to the buyer, at which time the risk of loss or damage to the goods generally passes from the seller to the buyer.

ex ship sales term denoting that the seller is responsible for arranging and paying for the carriage of the goods to the agreed port of destination where the buyer is responsible for their discharge from the ship. The risk of loss or damage to the goods generally passes from seller to buyer when the ship has arrived at the discharge port and the goods are available for unloading.

ex works sales term denoting that the seller is responsible for making the goods available at his works or factory. The buyer bears the cost of loading the goods on to the vehicle(s) and delivering them to the destination. The risk of loss or damage to the goods generally passes from the seller to the buyer from the time that they are made available.

excepted period period during which any time used to load or discharge does not count for the purpose of calculating demurrage or despatch, other than by prior agreement (*see* **unless used**). Such periods must be expressly stated in the charter-party and may include week-ends, public holidays and time used shifting from anchorage to berth. It should be noted that, once laytime has expired, time counts during excepted periods in the calculation of demurrage.

exception notation on a bill of lading made by the master, first officer or protection and indemnity club surveyor stating the condition of goods which, when loaded on to the ship, are not in apparent good order and condition.

exceptions clause   clause in a charter-party or bill of lading which exonerates the carrying ship from responsibility for damage to cargo from certain named causes such as an act of God or negligence of the master.

excess landing   cargo landed in excess of the quantity on the ship's manifest.

expiry of laytime   moment when the time allowed in the charter-party for loading and/or discharging, as the case may be, has been used up. If loading or discharging has not been completed, demurrage or damages for detention become payable.

explosimeter   instrument used to detect the presence of flammable gases in the tanks of a tanker.

extend a cancelling date (to)   to agree to a later date than that already agreed in the charter-party by which a ship must tender notice of readiness to the charterer that she has arrived and is ready to load. If a ship is likely to be delayed in reaching the load port, the shipowner may ask the charterer to extend the cancelling date. If the charterer agrees, the contract is amended accordingly. If not, the charterer may have the option to cancel the charter either before the cancelling date by mutual consent or after the cancelling date within a time specified in the charter-party. Alternatively, the shipowner may be obliged to present his ship at the load port, however late.

extend a charter (to)   to prolong the period during which a ship is on time charter. An option to extend the charter may be incorporated into the charter-party, very often on the same terms but possibly at a different rate of hire.

extend suit time (to)   as carrier, to extend the period within which cargo interests must bring a lawsuit for any claim which they have under the contract of carriage. Suit time may be extended at the request of cargo interests when the claim has not been fully quantified and provides the parties with further time to settle the claim out of court.

extension of a charter   prolonging of the period during which a ship is on time charter. *For further definition, see* **extend a charter (to)** *above.*

extension to the cancelling date   agreement by the charterer to a later date than that agreed in the charter-party by which a ship must tender notice of readiness to the charterer that she has arrived and is ready to load. *For further definition, see* **extend a cancelling date (to)** *above*.

extension to suit time   an extension by the carrier of the period within which cargo interests must bring a lawsuit for any claim which they have under the contract of carriage. This extension may be granted at the request of cargo interests when the claim has not been fully quantified and provides the parties with further time to settle the claim out of court.

extreme breadth   maximum breadth of a ship measured from the outsides of her plating.

F

f.   fresh.

f.a.c.   (1) *see* **forwarding agent's commission**.

f.a.c.   (2) *see* **fast as can** *below*.

f.a.c.c.o.p.   fast as can, custom of the port. *For definition, see* **fast as can** *and* **custom of the port**.

f.a.f.   fuel adjustment factor. *See* **fuel oil surcharge**.

fairlead   fitting in the deck of a ship which guides the ropes when the ship is being moored.

fairway   navigable channel.

f.a.k.   *see* **freight all kinds**.

f.a.s.   free alongside or free alongside ship. *For definition, see* **free alongside ship**.

fast as can   term used in a contract of carriage, particularly in those of shipping lines, to denote that the shipper must supply the cargo as fast as the ship can load or that the receiver must take delivery as fast as the ship can discharge.

f. & c.c.   *see* **full and complete cargo**.

f.c.l.   *see* **full container load.**

f.c.l. allowance   *see under* **full container load.**

f.c.l./f.c.l.   *see under* **full container load.**

f.c.l./l.c.l.   *see under* **full container load.**

f.d.   (1) *see* **free despatch.**

f.d.   (2) *see* **free discharge.**

f.d. & d.   *see* **freight, demurrage and defence.**

feeder   wooden box, open at the bottom, which is built under the hatchway of a ship when grain in bulk is to be carried. The grain is loaded into the cargo compartment filling the feeder which feeds the hold with grain as the cargo settles during the voyage, in order to prevent it from shifting.

feeder service   service provided by a shipping line whereby small ships carry cargoes regularly between ports which are served by a large ocean ship and ports which are not, for the reason that cargoes to and from these ports are not sufficient to warrant putting in a large ship but are transhipped to or from that ship. Normally, the shipping line charges a through rate of freight which includes the cost of transhipment.

feeder ship   small ship, provided by a shipping line, which carries cargoes between ports which are served by a large ocean ship and ports which are not. The cargoes are transhipped, normally at the expense of the shipping line, to or from the ocean ship.

Ferticon   voyage charter-party used for shipments of fertilizer, published by the Chamber of Shipping of the United Kingdom. The full name of this charter-party is the Chamber of Shipping Fertilizers Charter.

Fertivoy   voyage charter-party used for shipments of fertilizer from the United States of America and Canada. The full name of this charter-party is the North American Fertilizer Charter Party.

f.e.u.   *see* **forty foot equivalent unit.**

f.h.e.x.   *see* **Fridays and holidays excepted.**

fighting rate   freight rate introduced by a liner conference in order to eliminate competition by non-conference lines.

f.i.l.o.   *see* **free in liner out.**

f.i.l.t.d.   free in liner terms discharge. *See* **free in liner out.**

f.i.o.   *see* **free in and out.**

f.i.o.l.s. & d.   *see* **free in and out, lashed, secured and dunnaged.**

f.i.o.s.   *see* **free in and out and stowed.**

f.i.o.t.   *see* **free in and out and trimmed.**

firm offer   an offer which is not conditional in any way and is binding on the party making it, provided that it is accepted in full and within any time limit specified in it.

first class ship   ship to which the highest class has been given by a classification society in accordance with its rules concerning construction and maintenance.

fix (to)   to conclude successfully negotiations resulting in the charter of a ship.

fixed end flatrack   flatrack whose ends are not collapsible. For this reason, it is suitable for a trade where it is unlikely to be empty.

fixed on subjects   said of a ship, when the terms and conditions of chartering her have been agreed except for a few, normally minor, details.

fixture   successful conclusion of the negotiations between shipowner and charterer, generally through shipbrokers, resulting in the charter of a ship.

flag   nationality of a ship, that is, the country in which the ship is registered.

flag discrimination   action taken by the Government of a country to restrict all, or some proportion of, shipments, both imports and exports, to ships of that country's fleet. The main purpose is to build up or protect the fleet by providing it with employment. In some countries, this practice is designed to avoid spending foreign currencies. Very often, priority is given to cargo in a national flag ship or to the ship herself in the form of lower import duty, lower port charges or priority berthing. Some countries reserve coastal trade to their own ships.

flag of convenience   registration of a ship in a country whose tax on the profits of trading ships is low or whose requirements concerning manning or maintenance are not stringent. Sometimes referred to as a **flag of necessity**.

flag waiver   dispensation, given by a country which reserves the carriage of goods by sea to ships of its own national fleet, to ship goods in a ship of another nationality.

flash point   lowest temperature at which a product gives off an inflammable gas when mixed with air.

flat *or* **flatrack**   open flat bed on to which cargoes of awkward size, such as machinery, can be loaded for carriage in containerships. Flatracks have standard sizes and may have fixed ends or ends which collapse or fold flat so that, when empty, several may be interlocked in a stack which has the same dimensions as a standard shipping container, enabling them to be transported in the same way. When provided by an ocean carrier, this type of conveyance is sometimes the subject of an additional charge on the freight rate.

flight of locks   series of locks placed near to each other to convey ships to a much higher or lower level. *See also* **lock**.

floating crane   floating platform on which a crane is mounted. It is capable of being moved to any part of the port where it is required and very often has the capacity to handle heavy lifts.

floating dock   floating structure used for repairing ships out of the water. It is capable of being partially submerged to enable the ships to enter and leave.

flotsam   floating wreckage from a shipwreck.

flush tween hatch cover   hatch cover in the tween deck which does not protrude above the deck, thus enabling vehicles, such as fork-lift trucks, to move about easily.

f.o.   (1) *see* **free out**.

f.o.   (2) fuel oil.

f.o.b.   *see* **free on board**.

56

f.o.b. charges   *see under* **free on board.**

folding flatrack   shipping container, consisting of a flat bed and solid ends but with open sides, designed to carry cargoes of awkward size. When these flatracks are empty, the ends are folded down and several flatracks may then be interlocked in a stack which has the same dimensions as a single standard container enabling them to be transported in the same way.

f.o.q.   *see* **free on quay.**

f.o.r.   *see* **free on rail.**

force ice (to)   to use the weight of a ship to penetrate ice. Charter-parties often contain a clause stipulating that the ship shall not be required by the charterer to force ice.

force majeure   circumstance which is beyond the control of one of the parties to a contract and which may, according to the terms and conditions, relieve that party of liability for failing to execute the contract.

forced ventilation   system of ventilating the holds of a ship whereby ventilators on deck are closed off and air is circulated mechanically through the holds, being dried, if necessary, by dehumidifying equipment. This method of ventilating is useful when the outside air contains a high level of humidity which would cause condensation damage to the cargo if introduced into the holds. This system is also known as **mechanical ventilation**.

fore and aft stowage   stowage along the length of a ship, as opposed to stowage athwartships.

fore peak tank   small tank situated at the extreme forward end of a ship. It normally holds water ballast and is used to help to trim the ship, that is, to adjust the draughts forward and aft.

forecastle   raised part of the forward end of a ship's hull.

forest products carrier   ship designed for the carriage of timber, usually geared and having large hatchways. Also referred to as a **timber carrier**.

fork-lift pockets   openings in, for example, a shipping container into which the forks of a fork-lift truck can be inserted for lifting purposes.

fork-lift truck   vehicle used to move goods around a port or warehouse or within a ship. It is equipped with two horizontal prongs which penetrate special pockets on containers or the underside of pallets or between goods separated by dunnage. The prongs, known as forks, are power driven and can be raised and lowered as required.

forty foot equivalent unit unit of measurement equivalent to one forty foot container, normally abbreviated to **f.e.u.** Thus two twenty foot containers comprise an f.e.u. This measurement is used to quantify, for example, the container capacity of a ship, the number of containers carried on a particular voyage or over a period of time, or it may be the unit on which freight is based.

forward at or towards the bow or front of a ship.

forwarding agent *or* **forwarder** person or company who arranges the carriage of goods and the associated formalities on behalf of a shipper. The duties of a forwarding agent include booking space on a ship, providing all the necessary documentation and arranging Customs clearance. Also referred to as a **freight forwarder**.

forwarding agent's commission commission payable by a shipping line to a forwarding agent for obtaining cargoes. It is a percentage, varying from one line to another, of the freight.

f.o.s. *see* **fuel oil surcharge**.

f.o.t. free on truck. *For definition, see* **free on rail** *below*.

foul bill of lading bill of lading containing one, or more than one, superimposed clause specifying a defect to the cargo or packing, noted at the time the goods are received by the ship. Such a bill of lading is also referred to as dirty or unclean.

f.o.w. first open water.

f.p. (1) *see* **free pratique**.

f.p. (2) *see* **flash point**.

f.p.t. *see* **fore peak tank**.

frame one of a series of bars, often bulb flats, attached to the keel of a ship and supporting the plating at the sides of the ship.

franco domicile   *see* **free delivered** *below.*

free alongside ship   sales term denoting that the seller is responsible for bringing the goods alongside the ship at the loading port berth and on the date specified by the buyer, after which the risk of loss or damage to the goods generally passes from the seller to the buyer.

free delivered   sales term denoting that the seller is responsible for arranging and paying for the carriage of the goods to the place agreed in the contract. The seller bears the risk of loss or damage to the goods until they are delivered to that place. The contract should specify whether it is the buyer's or seller's responsibility to arrange Customs clearance and pay any import duty. Also referred to as **franco domicile** or, simply, **delivered**.

free despatch   provision in a voyage charter-party that despatch money is not payable when loading and/or discharging has been completed in less than the time allowed.

free discharge   term qualifying the freight rate in a voyage charter which signifies that the shipowner does not pay for the cost of discharging the cargo, but that this cost is to be borne by cargo interests, that is, the charterer or receiver, as the case may be.

free flow system   system employed in large tankers carrying one grade of cargo only whereby oil flows from one compartment to another through sluice gates, rather than having complex pipelines.

free in   free of expense to the shipowner of cargo handling at the loading port.

free in and out   term qualifying a freight rate which signifies that it excludes the cost of loading and discharging and, if appropriate to the type of cargo, stowing, dunnaging, lashing and securing or trimming, all of which are payable by the charterer or shipper or receiver, as the case may be. This type of rate is typically found in voyage charter-parties and, since the shipowner has no control over loading and discharging, these generally have suitable clauses for laytime and demurrage to allow for delays at the loading and discharging ports.

free in and out and stowed   qualification to a freight rate which is equivalent to **free in and out** but which avoids any ambiguity by specifying that the cost of stowage is not for the account of the shipowner. It is normally payable by the charterer or the shipper. *See also* **free in and out** *above.*

free in and out and trimmed   qualification to a freight rate which is equivalent to **free in and out** but which avoids any ambiguity by specifying that the cost of trimming is not for the account of the shipowner. It is normally payable by the charterer or the shipper. *See also* **free in and out**.

free in and out, lashed, secured and dunnaged qualification to a freight rate which is equivalent to **free in and out** but which avoids any ambiguity by specifying that the cost of lashing, securing and dunnaging is not for the account of the shipowner. It is normally payable by the charterer or the shipper. *See also* **free in and out**.

free in liner out *or* **free in liner terms discharge** qualification to a freight rate denoting that it is inclusive of the sea carriage and the cost of discharging. It excludes the cost of loading and, if appropriate to the type of cargo, stowing, dunnaging, lashing and securing or trimming, all of which are payable by the charterer or the shipper. This type of freight rate may have a provision for laytime and demurrage at the port of loading since the carrier has no control over the loading.

free on board sales term denoting that the seller is responsible for delivering the goods to the port of loading agreed in the contract and for loading them on to the ship nominated by the buyer. The risk of loss or damage to the goods generally passes from seller to buyer when the goods pass ship's rail at the port of loading.

    f.o.b. charges cargo handling charges levied on the shipper by the shipping line at the port of loading.

free on quay sales term denoting that the seller is responsible for delivering the goods onto the quay at the port of loading as near as possible to the ship nominated by the buyer.

free on rail *or* **free on truck** sales term denoting that the seller is responsible for delivering goods into the custody of the railway at a named place and, if agreed in the contract of sale, for loading into rail cars, at which time the risk of loss or damage to the goods generally passes from seller to buyer.

free out qualification to a freight rate denoting that the cost of discharging the cargo from the ship's hold is not included in the freight but is payable by the charterer or shipper or bill of lading holder, as the case may be. When qualifying a term of sale, it denotes that the purchase price of the goods does not include this cost which is borne by the buyer. Often, daily rates of discharging and demurrage are incorporated into such contracts.

free port separate area within a port where goods which have been imported may be held without payment of duty. Such goods are normally re-exported, sometimes after having been processed in some way.

free pratique   permission granted by the authorities at a port, being satisfied as to the state of health of those on board a ship on arrival, for them to make physical contact with the shore. Also referred to simply as **pratique**. A ship which is the subject of such permission is said to be **in free pratique**.

free time   period between the time a ship is ready to load or discharge, having given notice of readiness, and the time laytime commences in accordance with the charter-party, during which the charterer or receiver is not obliged to load or discharge. It is important to make a provision in the charter-party for the effect on laytime should the charterer or receiver elect to load or discharge during this period.

freeboard   distance between the deck line, that is, the line representing the uppermost continuous deck, and the relevant load line, painted on the side of a ship. Freeboards are assigned by a government department or, if authorized by that department, a classification society.

freight   (1) amount of money paid to a shipowner or shipping line for the carriage of cargo. Depending on the type of contract, the particular terms and, in some cases, the custom of the ports involved, the freight may include the cost of loading and/or discharging the cargo or may simply cover the ocean carriage. *For examples, see* **liner terms** *and* **free in and out**.

freight   (2) sometimes used to denote cargo.

freight (to)   (1) to determine or calculate the freight for a particular consignment.

freight (to)   (2) to show the freight (amount) on a document such as a ship's manifest.

freight (to)   (3) to hire out a ship.

freight account   invoice, rendered by a shipping line or shipowner to a shipper or charterer, showing the full amount of freight payable and the method by which this amount is arrived at, depending on the terms of the contract of carriage. The account includes any applicable surcharges and commission.

freight all kinds   single freight rate which is charged irrespective of the commodity.

freight canvasser   person who seeks out cargoes from shippers on behalf of a shipping line.

freight collect   freight payable at destination. Also referred to as **freight forward**.

freight conference   *see* **conference**.

freight, demurrage and defence   class of insurance provided by a protection and indemnity club which covers legal costs incurred by a shipowner in connection with claims arising from the operation of his ship.

freight forward   freight payable at destination. Also referred to as **freight collect**.

freight forwarder   person or company who arranges the carriage of goods and the associated formalities on behalf of a shipper. The duties of a freight forwarder include booking space on a ship, providing all the necessary documentation and arranging Customs clearance. Also referred to as a **forwarder** or **forwarding agent**.

freight payable at destination   method of paying the freight often used for shipments of bulk cargoes whose weight is established on discharge from the ship.

freight prepaid   freight which is payable before the contract has been performed. Very often, the bills of lading are signed and exchanged with the shipper for his payment of freight.

freight quotation   freight quoted by a shipping line or liner conference which may be given as an indication only.

freight rate   amount of money paid to a shipowner or shipping line for the carriage of each unit of cargo, such as a tonne, a cubic metre or container load. Also referred to as a **rate of freight**.

freight tariff   schedule, published by a liner conference or shipping line, containing freight rates for a variety of commodities likely to be carried by the line or lines and whether these are payable on the weight of the commodity or its cubic measurement. The tariff also contains details of charges for heavy lifts and long length cargoes, and terminal handling charges. Apart from matters of rating, the tariff of a liner conference states the geographical areas served, the names of the member lines and the conference's general regulations.

freight ton   unit of cargo on which a freight rate is based, generally one tonne or one cubic metre.

freighted manifest   manifest which details the freight charged against each bill of lading. This type of manifest is a requirement of certain importing countries.

freighter   a ship used for the carriage of cargo.

fresh water allowance   extra draught allowed by the load line regulations for loading in fresh water. This is because a ship's draught will be reduced when reaching the open sea where the density of water is greater.

fresh water freeboard   distance between the deck line and the appropriate load line for a ship in fresh water.

fresh water load line   line painted on the sides of a ship which shows the maximum depth to which a ship's hull may be immersed when in fresh water. The line is marked F. *See also* **load line zone**.

fresh water timber freeboard   distance between the deck line and the appropriate load line for a ship in fresh water with a deck cargo of timber.

fresh water timber load line   line painted on the sides of a ship which shows the maximum depth to which a ship's hull may be immersed when in fresh water with a deck cargo of timber. The line is marked LF. *See also* **load line zone**.

Fridays and holidays excepted   charter-party term which provides that Fridays and public holidays do not count in the calculation of laytime. This term applies to those countries where Friday is the Sabbath, notably in the Middle East. *See also* **even if used** *and* **unless used**.

frt.   *see* **freight**.

fuel oil surcharge *or* **fuel adjustment factor**   extra charge applied by a shipping line or liner conference to reflect fluctuations in the cost of bunkers. This surcharge is expressed either as an amount per freight ton or as a percentage of the freight. Also referred to as a **bunker surcharge** *or* **bunker adjustment factor**.

full and complete cargo   a quantity of cargo sufficient to fill a ship to capacity either by weight or cubic measurement.

full and down   said of a ship whose holds are full of cargo and whose hull is immersed as far as the permitted load line.

full container load   quantity of cargo which fills a shipping container to capacity, either by weight or cubic measurement.
  f.c.l. allowance   deduction from the f.c.l. freight provided by a shipping line or liner conference to a shipper who loads a minimum number of tonnes or cubic metres of cargo into a shipping container. There may be various allowances depending on the degree of utilization of the container. Also known as a **utilization allowance**.

  f.c.l./f.c.l.   term used to describe a container freight rate whereby the shipper is responsible for the packing of the container and the shipper or receiver, as the case may be, for the unpacking.

  f.c.l./l.c.l.   term used to describe a container freight rate whereby the shipper is responsible for the packing of the container and the carrier for the unpacking.

full liner terms   qualification to a freight rate which signifies that it consists of the ocean carriage and the cost of cargo handling at the loading and discharging ports, according to the custom of those ports. This varies widely from country to country and, within countries, from port to port: in some ports, the freight excludes all cargo handling costs while in others, the cost of handling between the hold and the ship's rail or quay is included in the freight.

f.w.   fresh water. This abbreviation is frequently used when qualifying a ship's cargo capacity when drawing a certain number of feet or metres in fresh water. For example, a ship might be said to be able to lift 12,500 tonnes on 26ft. f.w.

f.w.a.   *see* **fresh water allowance**.

G

g.a.   *see* **general average**.

gang   set of dockers. The number in a gang varies according to the size of ship being loaded or discharged, the type of cargo and the port.

gantry crane   overhead crane which travels on rails to enable it to be moved along the quay as required.

gas free (to) to remove gas from the cargo compartments of a tanker or combination carrier by ventilation after the cargo has been pumped out and the tank washed. Also said of tank containers.

gas oil type of oil used in light diesel engines.

gas-free said of the cargo compartments of a tanker or combination carrier once any gas has been expelled by ventilation, after the cargo has been pumped out and the holds or tanks washed. Also said of tank containers.

gas-free certificate document supplied by a suitably qualified person certifying that gases remaining in a cargo compartment or tank container, after the cargo has been discharged, have been removed.

Gasvoy voyage charter-party used for shipments of liquid gas, other than liquid natural gas, published by the Baltic and International Maritime Conference (B.I.M.C.O.).

geared ship ship which is equipped with her own crane(s) or derrick(s). Such a ship is required for a voyage where the loading or discharging port does not have shore cranes or, if available, where shore cranes are of insufficient lifting capacity or inefficient.

gearless ship ship which is not equipped with her own crane(s) or derrick(s). When chartering or scheduling such a ship for a particular voyage, it is necessary to ensure that the loading and discharging ports have shore cranes capable of lifting up to the heaviest piece weight of the ship's cargo.

Gencon general purpose voyage charter-party published by the Baltic and International Maritime Conference (B.I.M.C.O.).

general arrangement plan plan containing detailed drawings of a ship showing cargo and other compartments and lifting gear.

general average intentional act or sacrifice which is carried out during a voyage to preserve the venture from a real peril. The party who has suffered a loss as a result is reimbursed by all the other parties to the marine adventure, each paying a proportion of the amount of the loss according to the value of their interest.

general average act intentional act, authorized by the master of a ship, which is intended to preserve the voyage from a real peril and which results in a general

65

average loss. Such an act might be the putting out of a fire in a hold which causes cargo to be damaged by water.

general average clause   clause in a bill of lading or charter-party which stipulates in what country or place and by what rules, often the York-Antwerp Rules, general average is to be adjusted.

general average contribution   monetary contribution to a party suffering a general average loss from each of the parties to the voyage. The amount of each party's contribution is based on the proportion which that party's property bears to the total value of all the property in the voyage.

general average sacrifice   intentional act, authorized by the master of a ship, which is intended to preserve the voyage from a real peril and which results in a general average loss. Such an act might be the jettison of cargo to lighten a ship which is aground and in danger of breaking up if not refloated.

general cargo   cargo consisting of goods unpacked or packed, for example, in cartons, crates, bags or bales, often palletized, but not in shipping containers.

general cargo ship   ship designed to carry general cargo. Used widely in the liner trade, it is usual for this type of ship to have several decks because of the number of ports served and the range of products carried.

general purpose container   shipping container suitable for general cargo. It is normally made of steel and cargo is loaded into it, and discharged from it, at the rear where it can be closed by means of two doors. There are several standard sizes for this type of container but the most widely used world-wide are the twenty foot and forty foot containers.

general purpose rating   seaman who can work as a deck or engine-room rating.

general rate increase   periodic increase to all the base freight rates in the tariff of a liner conference or shipping line.

generals   short form of general cargo. *For definition, see* **general cargo** *above.*

Genorecon   general ore voyage charter-party published by the Baltic and International Maritime Conference (B.I.M.C.O.).

geographical rotation   sequence in which a ship calls at the ports on her itinerary utilizing the most direct route, that is, by not passing any of the ports while en route to another.

Germancon-North (1) voyage charter-party, published by the Baltic and International Maritime Conference (B.I.M.C.O.), used for shipments of coal, coke and patent fuel from the Ruhr to all ports in Denmark, Finland, Norway and Sweden.

Germancon-North (2) bill of lading intended to be used for shipments of coal, coke or patent fuel from the Ruhr to all ports in Denmark, Finland, Norway and Sweden under the Germancon-North charter-party.

Germanischer Lloyd West German ship classification society. *For the functions of a ship classification society, see* **classification society**.

G.L. Germanischer Lloyd—West German ship classification society. *See also* **classification society**.

g.m. metacentric height, that is, the distance between the centre of gravity of a ship (g.) and her metacentre (m.). *See also* **metacentric height**.

G.M.T. Greenwich Mean Time.

g.o. *see* **gas oil**.

go back (to) said of a ship, to have an estimated date or time of arrival, readiness or completion of loading or discharging, as the case may be, which is later than previously advised or expected. Also referred to as **to drop back**.

g.p. general purpose. *See* **general purpose container** *and* **general purpose rating** *above*.

gr. grain. *See* **grain (capacity)**.

grab mechanical device, attached to a crane, used to discharge some types of bulk cargo. It lifts cargo by gripping.

grab damage damage to a ship caused by the use of mechanical grabs which are employed to discharge some types of bulk cargo.

grain (capacity) total cubic capacity of a ship's holds available for the carriage of grain or any other free-flowing bulk cargo which is capable of filling the space between the ship's frames. It is expressed in cubic feet or cubic metres.

Grainvoy   voyage charter-party used for shipments of grain.

Grainvoybill   bill of lading intended to be used for shipments of grain under the Grainvoy charter-party.

graving dock   enclosed basin from which all the water is pumped to enable ships to be surveyed and repaired while out of the water. Also referred to as a **dry dock**.

greaser   engine-room rating.

great circle route   shortest route between two points.

g.r.i.   *see* **general rate increase**.

gross register tonnage *or* **gross registered tonnage**   *see* **gross tonnage**.

gross terms   type of voyage charter in which the shipowner pays for loading and discharging.

gross tonnage   the total of all the enclosed spaces within a ship, expressed in tons each of which is equivalent to one hundred cubic feet. Also referred to as **gross register tonnage** and **gross registered tonnage**.

gross weight   weight of goods and their packing.

ground (to)   to touch the bottom.

grounding   deliberate contact by a ship with the bottom while the ship is moored or anchored as a result of the water level dropping.

groupage   the grouping together of several compatible consignments into a full container load. Also referred to as **consolidation**.

groupage bill of lading   bill of lading, issued by a carrier to a forwarding agent, which covers consignments from various shippers for the same destination which have been consolidated into one consignment by the forwarding agent. Each shipper receives a house bill of lading from the forwarding agent covering his consignment.

g.r.t.   gross register tonnage or gross registered tonnage. *For definition, see* **gross tonnage** *above.*

H

ha. *see* **hatch** *and* **hatchway.**

Hague Rules   rules governing the carriage of goods by sea and identifying the rights and responsibilities of carriers and owners of cargo. These rules were published in 1924 following an international convention and were subsequently given the force of law by many maritime nations.

Hague-Visby Rules   set of rules, amending the Hague Rules (*see above*), published in 1968 and subsequently given the force of law by many maritime nations.

half despatch   term used in a voyage charter-party stipulating that despatch money, that is, the amount payable to the charterer, shipper or receiver, as the case may be, by the shipowner for loading and/or discharging in less than the time allowed in the charter-party, is to be calculated at half the agreed rate of demurrage.

half height container   shipping container which has a standard length and width but only half the height. It is suitable for the carriage of dense cargoes since these take up a relatively small space in relation to their weight. Two half height containers occupy one cell in a containership. These types of containers often have an open top with a waterproof cover since many of the cargoes are loaded from the top.

half hire   provision in a time charter-party that half the amount of daily hire is payable under certain circumstances. For example, if a ship is lost at sea, it may be agreed that half hire is payable from the date when the ship was last heard from until the calculated date of arrival at her destination.

Hamburg Rules   rules governing the rights and responsibilities of carrier and cargo interests which may be incorporated into a contract for the carriage of goods by sea either by agreement of the parties or statutorily. These rules were adopted by the United Nations Convention on the Carriage of Goods by Sea in 1978.

harbour   a natural or artificial shelter for ships.

harbour dues   charge levied against a shipowner or ship operator by a port authority for the use of a harbour.

hatch   widely used short form for hatch cover. *For definition, see* **hatch cover**

below. Also frequently used to mean hatchway. *For this definition, see* **hatchway** *below*.

hatch beam   steel beam, one of several laid across the hatchway of a ship, on which the hatch cover rests when the hatchway is closed.

hatch boards   wooden boards used to cover the hatchway of a ship. This method of closing a hatchway has been largely replaced by the use of steel hatch covers.

hatch coaming   steel surround to a hatchway which rises vertically from the deck of a ship. Its functions are to prevent water from entering the hold and to lessen the risk of any person who may be working on the deck falling through the open hatchway. Also referred to simply as a **coaming**.

hatch cover   means of closing the hatchway of a ship. There are various types, for example, wooden boards laid across the hatchway or steel sections which roll to one end or one side. Sometimes referred to as a **hatch**.

hatch list   list of all the bills of lading, together with brief details of the goods, stowed in each of the holds of a ship.

hatchway   opening in the deck of a ship through which cargo is loaded into, or discharged from, the hold, and which is closed by means of a hatch cover. A hatchway is sometimes referred to as a **hatch**.

head   bows or forward part of a ship. A ship is said to be **down by the head** if her draught forward is deeper than her draught aft.

head charter *or* **head charter-party**   contract for the charter of a ship, between her owner and a charterer. This term is used to distinguish between this charter-party and any contract which the charterer may have with a third party to whom he sub-lets the ship.

head charterer   charterer whose contract is direct with the shipowner in respect of a ship which is being chartered out and then sub-chartered, perhaps several times. The head charterer is thus distinguished from all the sub-charterers.

heating coil   device fitted in the tank of a tanker which, by means of steam, maintains viscous cargoes, such as bitumen or heavy oil, in a liquid state and capable of being pumped out.

heave to (to)   to bring a ship to a stop.

heavy lift   generally, a lift which requires special lifting equipment by virtue of its weight. When carried by a shipping line, a heavy lift may be described as any lift which exceeds a specific weight as stated in the line's tariff and which is normally the subject of a heavy lift additional charge.

heavy lift additional   extra charge applied by a liner conference or a shipping line on lifts exceeding a weight specified in its tariff, often five tonnes. Also referred to as a **heavy lift surcharge**.

heavy lift ship   ship designed to lift and carry exceptionally heavy loads such as railway locomotives. These are loaded and discharged by means of a heavy lift derrick fixed to the deck of the ship.

heavy lift surcharge   *see* **heavy lift additional** *above.*

heavy weather   severe weather giving rise to the possibility of damage to a cargo at sea. If a ship encounters heavy weather, her master may note protest on arrival at the next port of call, which may be a necessity in order to avoid liability for damage to cargo.

heel (to)   said of a ship, to lean to one side temporarily.

h.f.o.   heavy fuel oil.

hire (money)   money paid by a charterer to a shipowner for the hire of a ship taken on time charter. It may be expressed, for example, as an amount per day or per deadweight tonne per month. Hire is payable, by agreement, at regular intervals such as monthly or semi-monthly, normally in advance. It is important that hire money is paid on time since otherwise the shipowner has the right to withdraw the ship from the service of the charterer.

hire statement   written statement of the amount of hire money payable by a time charterer to a shipowner, showing the number of days which have elapsed since the commencement of the charter or since the last statement. Deductions may be made for items disbursed by the charterer on behalf of the shipowner, such as cash advanced to the master; claims against the shipowner and off hire periods are also often deducted. The first and last statements detail the quantity of bunkers on board at the time of delivery and redelivery respectively of the ship, and corresponding adjustments made to the amounts of the remittances to take account of the purchase of bunkers on board on delivery by the charterer and the subsequent sale of bunkers on board on redelivery to the shipowner.

71

ho.   *see* **hold.**

hog (to)   said of a ship, to be loaded in such a way that the ends of the ship are depressed below the level of the centre. This bending of the ship's plating may result in damage or distortion.

hold   space below the deck of a ship, used to carry cargo. The holds of a ship are numbered one and upwards from the forward to the after end for the purposes of their identification and the location of cargo.

hold cleaning   making a hold clean after one cargo has been discharged and before the next one is loaded. This work is normally carried out by the crew of the ship and is one example of customary assistance given by a master and crew to a time charterer.

home port   place from where a ship is operated.

home trade ship *or* **home trader**   ship which is engaged in home trade voyages the scope of which varies from country to country but which generally consists of a country's coastline and those neighbouring coastlines which enable the ship to stay close to land. Such ships are permitted to trade with fewer crew than a foreign-going ship.

homogeneous cargo   entire cargo which is of one kind.

hose test (to)   to test a hatch cover for watertightness by spraying with a hose.

house bill of lading   bill of lading issued by a forwarding agent to a shipper covering a consignment which the forwarding agent has grouped with consignments from other shippers to the same destination. The forwarding agent receives one groupage bill of lading from the carrier which covers all the consignments.

house flag   ship's flag bearing the emblem of the shipowner or shipping line. Some time charter-parties allow the charterer to fly his house flag during the period of the charter.

house to house   said of a service or freight rate provided by a container shipping line whereby goods are loaded into a shipping container at the shipper's premises and not unloaded until they arrive at the consignee's premises. Also referred to as **door to door.**

h.p.   horse power.

h.s.s.   heavy grain, sorghum and soya.

husbandry   maintenance and repair of a ship.

h.w.   high water.

h.w.o.n.t.   high water ordinary neap tides.

h.w.o.s.t.   high water ordinary spring tides.

hygroscopic cargo   cargo which is capable of absorbing moisture, for example, from the atmosphere, and can accordingly suffer a change of weight during an ocean passage.

I

I.A.C.S.   *see* **International Association of Classification Societies.**

i.a.f.   *see* **inflation adjustment factor.**

i.c.d.   inland container depot.

ice class ship   ship which has been suitably strengthened in accordance with the rules of a ship classification society, for navigation in ice conditions of a particular severity.

ice clause   clause in a bill of lading or charter-party which sets out the options available to the parties to the contract of carriage in the event that navigation is prevented or temporarily delayed by severe ice conditions. The wording of the clause and the options vary according to the individual contract: a master may have the right to divert the ship to the nearest safe port to discharge cargo destined for an ice-bound port. Equally, a charterer may have the option of keeping a ship waiting for ice conditions to clear on payment of demurrage.

ice-bound   (1) said of a port which is inaccessible to shipping because of severe ice conditions. Provision is usually made in a bill of lading or charter-party for the course of action or options available to the parties to the contract of carriage in the event that the port of loading or discharging is ice-bound.

ice-bound   (2) said of a ship which is unable to leave a port or place because of severe ice conditions.

ice-breaker   ship whose hull is specially strengthened to enable her to crush ice using her own weight in order to make a passage sufficient for other ships to navigate.

ice-breaker assistance   the making of a passage or channel through ice by an ice-breaker enabling ships to reach open water or lighter ice conditions where they are able to navigate safely. *See also* **ice-breaker** *above.*

ice-strengthened ship   ship whose hull is strengthened to enable her to navigate in ice conditions: the shell plating is thicker and the bows reinforced.

identity of carrier clause   clause in a bill of lading which stipulates who the carrier is, that is, the party responsible for the care of the cargo under the terms of the contract of carriage. This is normally the shipowner since the party issuing the bill of lading may have chartered the ship and may not be responsible for the navigation of the ship nor for the handling of the cargo. There are some countries in which this clause may not be upheld.

idle   said of equipment or of a ship for which there is no work for a particular period of time.

i.f.o.   intermediate fuel oil.

i.g.s.   *see* **inert gas system.**

imbalance of trade   difference between the quantity of cargo shipped from one end of a trade route, or the revenue derived therefrom, and the quantity of cargo or revenue from the other end.

immediate rebate   discount on the freight rate offered by a liner conference to a shipper who has a loyalty contract with that conference. The contract requires the shipper to ship all his cargoes in the ships of member lines of the conference.

I.M.O.   *see* **International Maritime Organization.**

import entry   declaration to the Customs authorities of goods being imported to assess whether any duties or taxes are payable.

incorporation (of a surcharge)   the building in to a freight rate of part or all of a surcharge such as the currency adjustment factor or bunker surcharge.

Incoterms   rules governing the interpretation of terms used in international

74

trade, published by the International Chamber of Commerce. Against each of the terms of sale, such as f.o.b., c.i.f. and delivered, are defined the duties of buyer and seller. These rules are incorporated into a contract of sale by agreement of the two parties.

indemnity   compensation offered by one party to another for the consequences of carrying out, or omitting to carry out, a certain act. An indemnity is usually given in writing but is unenforceable in a court of law if the act for which it is given is intended to defraud an innocent third party.

independent line   shipping line which operates on a route served by a liner conference but which is not a member of that conference. Also referred to as a **non-conference line** or an **outsider**.

inducement   minimum quantity of cargo required by a shipping line to make it worthwhile to call at a particular port for loading or discharging.

inert gas system   system of preventing any explosion in the cargo tanks of a tanker by replacing the cargo, as it is pumped out, by an inert gas, often the exhaust of the ship's engine.

inflation adjustment factor   extra charge applied by a liner conference or a shipping line to cover costs affected by inflation in the country of shipment.

infrastructure (of a port)   equipment and services of a port.

inherent vice   natural failing of a product which leads to damage when it is subjected to certain conditions. An example is the susceptibility of some foods to perish. Carriers and insurance underwriters are not normally liable for damage caused in this way.

Institute Warranty Limits   geographical limits within which a ship may navigate without incurring any additional premium.

insufficient packing   failure of the packing to protect the goods while in transit. This may relieve the carrier and insurance underwriters of any liability for damage to cargo.

insulated container   shipping container which is lined so as to minimize the effects of changes in temperature on the cargo, thus reducing the likelihood of condensation. Such containers are suitable for goods which need protection from changes in temperature while not needing refrigeration.

intaken weight   actual weight of cargo loaded on board a ship.

Intankbill   bill of lading used for shipments under tanker voyage charter-parties.

Interclub Agreement   agreement between a number of major protection and indemnity clubs on the method of apportioning liability for loss or damage to cargo carried in ships chartered under a New York Produce Exchange charter-party.

Interconsec   document, published by the International Association of Independent Tanker Owners (Intertanko), containing clauses used for consecutive voyages under a tanker charter-party.

interim voyage   voyage undertaken by a ship between the time she is chartered for a specific voyage and the time she performs it.

intermodal tariff   tariff of freight rates of a shipping line or liner conference covering inland as well as ocean legs.

intermodal transport   carriage of a consignment of goods using more than one mode of transport, such as rail and sea.

International Association of Classification Societies   association of major classification societies whose principal aim is the improvement of standards of safety at sea.

International Load Line Certificate   certificate which gives details of a ship's freeboards and states that the ship has been surveyed and the appropriate load lines marked on her sides. This certificate is issued either by a government department or, if authorized by that department, a classification society. As required by the International Convention on Load Lines, the ship is surveyed periodically and the certificate renewed.

International Load Line Exemption Certificate   certificate exempting a ship from the requirements of the International Convention on Load Lines. An exemption may be given to a ship not normally involved in international voyages but which is to undertake a single such voyage.

International Maritime Organization   agency of the United Nations concerned with safety at sea. Its work includes codes and rules relating to tonnage measurement of ships, load lines and the safe carriage of grain. Its previous name was the Inter-Governmental Maritime Consultative Organization (I.M.C.O.).

International Tonnage Certificate   certificate issued to a shipowner by a government department in the case of a ship whose gross and net tonnages have been determined in accordance with the International Convention of Tonnage Measurement of Ships. The certificate states the gross and net tonnages together with details of the spaces attributed to each.

Intertanko   association of independent tanker owners whose aims are to represent the views of its members internationally and whose work includes the production of a number of standard documents, such as the Intertankvoy charter-party.

Intertankvoy   tanker voyage charter-party, published by the International Association of Independent Tanker Owners.

inward   relating to the arrival of a ship at a port. For example, an inward cargo is one which is arriving at a port for discharging there. A ship's inward charges are those incurred in entering a port, such as inward pilotage.

I.T.F.   International Transport Workers' Federation. Trade union, one of whose objects has been the setting of standards of employment for merchant seamen. Many prospective time charterers make it a stipulation of the charter that the shipowner meets the requirements of the I.T.F.

itinerary   list of all the ports at which a ship calls on a particular voyage to load and discharge cargo, often including the estimated arrival and sailing dates at each port. When incorporated into a set of instructions to the master of a ship for his next voyage, the itinerary may include ports where it is intended to take on bunkers.

I.W.L.   *see* **Institute Warranty Limits.**

J

jerque note   document given by the Customs authorities certifying that the inward clearance formalities for a ship have been completed.

jetsam   cargo jettisoned from a ship, that is, thrown overboard in order to lighten the ship, and washed ashore.

jettison the throwing overboard of cargo to lighten a ship so as to save the ship, her crew and remaining cargo from a peril. This action is often allowed as a general average sacrifice.

jettison (to) to throw cargo overboard to lighten a ship so as to save the ship, her crew and remaining cargo from a peril. *See also* **jettison** *above.*

jettison clause clause in a bill of lading or charter-party setting out the circumstances under which a master is entitled to jettison goods from a ship.

jetty structure, often of masonry, projecting out to sea, designed to protect a port from the force of the waves but also used to berth ships.

jib arm of a crane which extends outwards and from which hangs, at one end, the hook used for lifting goods.

joint service liner service operated by two or more shipping lines who jointly advertise their ships and canvass for cargo for a particular route. Unlike a consortium, there is no joint capital investment in ships or equipment.

joint survey inspection carried out by a surveyor on behalf of two parties, the cost generally being borne by both.

jumbo derrick derrick capable of lifting exceptionally heavy pieces of cargo. *See also* **derrick**.

jumboising conversion of a ship to increase cargo-carrying capacity by dividing her and adding a new section.

jurisdiction clause clause in a bill of lading or charter-party which stipulates that any dispute between the parties arising from the contract be resolved in a court of law, as opposed to arbitration. It also specifies which country has jurisdiction, that is, the authority to administer justice. Also known as the **litigation clause**.

K

keel longitudinal girder at the lowest point of a ship from which the framework is built up.

keel clearance minimum distance between the bottom of a ship and the bed of a river or sea, required by some authorities as a safety margin because of unseen hazards or climatic changes in the depth of water. Also known as **underkeel clearance**.

kg(s). kilogramme(s).

knot   measure of speed of a ship, equal to one nautical mile (6,080 feet or 1,852 metres) per hour.

kt.   abbreviation of knot. *For definition, see* **knot** *above.*

L

laden   loaded.

laden draught   depth of water to which a ship is immersed when fully loaded.

lagan   goods which have been jettisoned but attached to a floating object so that they can be recovered later.

laker   type of ship which trades only in the Great Lakes of North America, carrying mainly ore and grain.

Lamcon   voyage charter-party, published by the Baltic and International Maritime Conference (B.I.M.C.O.), used for shipments of iron ore from Liberia.

Lamconbill   bill of lading intended to be used for shipments of iron ore from Liberia under the Lamcon charter-party.

landbridge   overland portion of a voyage which links two portions made by sea.

landing charges   charges for putting cargo, which is being discharged from a ship, on to the quay.

landing, storage and delivery   charge, borne by cargo interests at some discharge ports, for putting the cargo on to the quay, taking it into storage and subsequently delivering ex store on to the consignee's vehicles.

lash   lighter aboard ship. *For definition, see* **barge-carrying ship**.

lash (to)   to hold goods in position by the use of, for example, wires, ropes, chains or straps.

lashing point   point on the deck of a ship, on a vehicle or inside a shipping container to which wires, chains, ropes or straps are attached which are used to hold goods in position.

latitude   distance North or South of the equator.

lay up (to)   to cease trading a ship temporarily during a period when there is a surplus of ships in relation to the level of available cargoes. *See also* **lay-up** *below.*

laycan   *see* **laydays cancelling.**

laydays   days allowed by the shipowner to the voyage charterer or bill of lading holder in which to load and/or discharge the cargo. *See also* **laytime** *below.*

laydays cancelling   period during which the shipowner must tender notice of readiness to the charterer that the ship has arrived at the port of loading and is ready to load. This period is expressed as two dates, for example, laydays 25 March cancelling 2 April or, when abbreviated to laycan, laycan 25 March/2 April. The charterer is not obliged to commence loading until the first of these dates if the ship arrives earlier and may have the option of cancelling the charter if the ship arrives after the second of the dates, known as the cancelling date.

laytime   time allowed by the shipowner to the voyage charterer or bill of lading holder in which to load and/or discharge the cargo. It is expressed as a number of days or hours or as a number of tonnes per day. There is normally a provision in the charter-party for the commencement of laytime, which is often at a certain hour after notice of readiness has been tendered by the master, a provision for periods when laytime does not count, for instance during bad weather, weekends or holidays and a provision for laytime being exceeded, when demurrage or damages for detention become payable, or not being fully used, when despatch money may be payable.

laytime saved   charter-party term used to define one method by which despatch money is calculated, that is, by deducting laytime used from laytime allowed. If, for example, a charter-party provides for six laydays for loading and the charterer uses $2\frac{1}{2}$ days, he is entitled to $3\frac{1}{2}$ days' despatch money. Also referred to as **working time saved**. *See* **all time saved** *for an alternative method of calculating despatch money.*

laytime statement portion of a time sheet which details the amount of laytime used by a voyage charterer.

lay-up temporary cessation of trading of a ship by a shipowner during a period when there is a surplus of ships in relation to the level of available cargoes. This surplus, known as over-tonnaging, has the effect of depressing freight rates to the extent that some shipowners no longer find it economical to trade their ships, preferring to lay them up until there is a reversal in the trend. During lay-up, the daily running cost of the ship is greatly reduced. Tankers, which have been laid up because of the surplus of ships, are sometimes used for storage of oil so as to reduce the losses suffered through not trading.

l.b.p. *see* **length between perpendiculars**.

l/c letter of credit.

l.c.l. *see* **less than container load**.

l.c.l./f.c.l. *see under* **less than container load**.

l.c.l./l.c.l. *see under* **less than container load**.

leg (of a voyage) one of a number of elements into which a ship's voyage is broken down. Generally, this is from one port of call to the next but may be any convenient sub-division to enable a shipowner or ship operator to evaluate the overall profitability of the ship or voyage. The legs of a voyage are also taken into account when assessing the quantity of bunkers required, since a ship may consume less when in ballast than when loaded.

length between perpendiculars length of a ship measured at a certain level between two perpendicular lines. The method of calculating this distance varies according to the particular classification society but, typically, is from the foremost point of the ship to the aftermost point or to the after side of the rudder post, measured at the ship's summer load line.

length overall maximum length between the extreme ends, forward and aft, of a ship.

less than container load consignment of cargo which is insufficient to fill a shipping container. It is grouped with other consignments for the same destination in a container at a container freight station.
> **l.c.l/f.c.l.** term used to describe a container freight rate whereby the carrier is responsible for the packing of the container and the shipper or receiver, as the case may be, for the unpacking.

l.c.l./l.c.l. term used to describe a container freight rate whereby the carrier is responsible for the packing and unpacking of the container.

letter of indemnity written statement in which one party undertakes to compensate another for the costs and consequences of carrying out a certain act. For example, a shipper who has been delayed in sending an original bill of lading to the receiver may instruct the master of the ship or the shipowner to release the goods to a named party without production of an original bill of lading. The master or owner, if they agree, may require a letter of indemnity from the shipper for the consequences of complying should it turn out that the named party is not entitled to take delivery of the goods. It should be noted that, as a rule, any such letter which seeks to indemnify against an act which is intended to defraud an innocent third party is unenforceable in a court of law.

lien the right to retain control of the property of another until a debt relating to it has been paid.

lien clause clause in a voyage charter-party which entitles the shipowner to exercise a lien on the cargo, that is, to retain control of the cargo until any freight, deadfreight or demurrage which is owing is paid. This provision is often incorporated into the cesser clause which seeks to relieve the charterer of all responsibility under the charter-party once the cargo has been shipped.

l.i.f.o. *see* **liner in free out.**

lift (1) weight of an individual piece of cargo lifted by a crane or derrick.

lift (2) weight of cargo capable of being carried by a ship, often based on a particular draught.

lift (to) (cargo) said of a ship, to load a particular weight of cargo, often based on a specific draught.

lift (to) (bunkers) to take bunkers on board.

lift-on lift-off system of loading and discharging, normally said of shipping containers, whereby cargo is lifted on and off a ship by cranes.

light displacement weight of a ship's hull, machinery, equipment and spares. This is often the basis on which ships are paid for when purchased for scrapping. The difference between the loaded displacement and light displacement is the ship's deadweight.

light dues   charge, levied against a ship, which contributes to the upkeep of a country's lighthouses.

lighten (to)   to remove cargo from a ship in order to reduce her draught. This operation may be carried out to enable a ship to clear a bar or sand-bank or to enter a port where the depth of water is otherwise insufficient.

lighter   type of barge used to carry to a port part of the cargo of an ocean ship. This operation is carried out, for example, when the draught of the ship is too deep to reach the port, sufficient cargo being discharged to lighters to reduce the draught.

lighterage   (1) the use of lighters or barges, very often for the purpose of carrying cargo discharged from an ocean ship in order to lighten her and reduce her draught.

lighterage   (2) monetary charge for the use of lighters or barges for the carriage of cargo.

limber board   removable board which is lifted to inspect a bilge.

limitation of liability   maximum sum of money payable by a carrier to a shipper or bill of lading holder for any damage or loss to the cargo for which the carrier is liable under the contract of carriage. The basis of the limitation may be per piece or package or per tonne or per container according to the particular contract. The amount of the limitation is determined by agreement of the two parties or by law.

line   abbreviation for shipping line, a company which operates a ship or ships on a regular basis between advertised ports and offers space for goods in return for freight based on a tariff of rates.

liner (ship)   cargo-carrying ship which is operated between scheduled, advertised ports of loading and discharge on a regular basis.

liner bill of lading   bill of lading containing the terms and conditions of carriage of a shipping line.

liner in free out   qualification to a freight rate denoting that it is inclusive of the sea carriage and the cost of loading. It excludes the cost of discharging which is payable by the shipper or receiver, as the case may be. There may be a laytime and demurrage arrangement at the port of discharging since the carrier has no control over the discharging.

liner service   service provided by a shipping company whereby cargo-carrying ships are operated between scheduled, advertised ports of loading and discharging on a regular basis. The freight rates which are charged are based on the shipping company's tariff or, if the company is a member of a liner conference, the tariff of that conference.

liner terms   qualification to a freight rate which signifies that it consists of the ocean carriage and the cost of cargo handling at the loading and discharging ports according to the custom of those ports. This varies widely from country to country and, within countries, from port to port: in some ports, the freight excludes all cargo handling costs while in others the cost of handling between the hold and the ship's rail or quay is included.

liner waybill   document, issued by a shipping line to a shipper, which serves as a receipt for the goods and evidence of the contract of carriage. In these respects it resembles a bill of lading but, unlike a bill of lading, it is not a document of title; it bears the name of the consignee who has only to identify himself in order to take delivery of the cargo. Because it is not negotiable, the liner waybill is not acceptable to banks as collateral security. The purpose of the liner waybill is to avoid the delays to ships and cargoes which occur when bills of lading are late in arriving at the discharge port. The liner waybill is also referred to as a **sea waybill** or an **ocean waybill** or simply a **waybill**.

Linertime   deep sea time charter-party, published by the Baltic and International Maritime Conference (B.I.M.C.O.), used when ships are chartered for liner operation.

liquid natural gas carrier *or* **liquefied natural gas carrier**   ship designed to carry natural gas (methane) in liquid form. This state is maintained by refrigeration.

liquid petroleum gas carrier *or* **liquefied petroleum gas carrier**   ship designed to carry liquid petroleum gas, such as butane or propane, by means of tanks within the holds. The gas is kept in liquid form by pressure and refrigeration.

list (to)   said of a ship, to lean over to one side.

litigation clause   clause in a bill of lading or charter-party which stipulates that any dispute between the parties arising from the contract be resolved in a court of law, as opposed to arbitration. It also specifies which country has jurisdiction, that is, the authority to administer justice. Also known as the **jurisdiction clause**.

l.l.a.   *see* **long length additional**.

Lloyd's Agents   members of a world-wide network of agents of Lloyd's of London, located at most of the large ports and many of the smaller ones. Their functions are to report to Lloyd's on shipping movements and casualties and to carry out surveys on behalf of insurance underwriters or cargo receivers.

Lloyd's Register of Shipping   British ship classification society. *For the functions of a ship classification society, see* **classification society**.

l.n.g.   liquid natural gas or liquefied natural gas.

l.o.a.   *see* **length overall**.

load   quantity or nature of what is being carried. This term normally refers to transport by truck.

load (to)   to place goods in a ship.

load displacement   *see* **loaded displacement**.

load line   one of the lines painted on the sides of a ship which show the maximum depths to which the ship may be immersed when arriving at, sailing through or putting to sea in the different load line zones. The positioning of these lines is determined by the rules agreed at the International Conference on Load Lines which have been ratified by many maritime countries.

load line mark   ring painted on the sides of a ship amidships bisected by a horizontal line which is level with the ship's summer load line.

load line zone   geographical area, defined by the International Conference on Load Lines, where a ship's hull may be immersed no deeper than the appropriate load line. There are five types of zone: tropical, summer, winter, seasonal tropical and seasonal winter. The first three types are permanent, that is, the one appropriate load line applies all year round. The last two being seasonal, the corresponding load lines apply at certain periods only, depending on the particular zone; for the rest of the year, the summer load line applies.

load ready   said of the date on which a ship is ready to load cargo.

loaded displacement *or* **load displacement**   weight of a ship's hull, machinery, equipment, spares, cargo, bunkers, fresh water and crew when the ship is immersed to her summer load line. The difference between the loaded displacement and the light displacement is the ship's deadweight.

loaded leg   sub-division of a ship's voyage during which the ship is carrying a cargo. It is useful for a shipowner or ship operator to break a voyage down into legs, both loaded and ballast, in order to determine the profitability of the voyage and to assess requirements for bunkers since a ship may consume more when loaded.

loading broker   company which represents a shipping line at the port of loading. Its duties are to advertise the line's sailings, to obtain cargoes and co-ordinate their delivery to the ship and to sign bills of lading on behalf of the master.

loading rights   authorization granted by all the member lines of a liner conference to a particular member line to load cargo on a regular basis at a certain port, coastline or country, as the case may be.

loadline *or* **load-line**   alternative spellings for load line. *For definition, see* **load line** *above*.

lock   space, enclosed at the sides by walls and at each end by gates, into which ships enter in order to be floated up or down to a different level or to gain access to, or to leave, an enclosed dock. Ships enter a lock through one gate and leave through the other one once sufficient water has been let in or out, as the case may be.

lock through (to)   to take a ship through a lock.

log (book)   book in which are recorded daily all events relating to the voyage of a ship, such as her position and speed and details of the weather.

log abstract   extract of a ship's log book. For example, abstracts which give details of the ship's speed and the weather conditions encountered at sea are normally available to a time charterer so that the ship's performance may be accurately calculated and compared with any warranty in the charter-party.

log carrier   ship designed to carry logs, usually geared and having long, wide hatchways.

lo-lo   *see* **lift-on lift-off**.

long length additional   extra charge applied by liner conferences and shipping lines on cargo exceeding a length specified in their tariff, often 40 feet or 12 metres. This extra charge is normally expressed as an amount of money per tonne for each unit of length, for example each foot, or part thereof in excess of the specified length.

long ton   2,240 lbs.

longitude   distance East or West of the Greenwich meridian.

longitudinal bulkhead   vertical separation in a ship which runs either along her entire length, such as the bulkhead which separates side tanks from centre tanks in a tanker, or along parts of the length, as with a centre-line bulkhead in a dry cargo ship which does not continue under the hatchways; this type of bulkhead is constructed to provide additional longitudinal strength.

longshoreman   dock worker, particularly in the United States of America.

loose   said of a consignment which consists of single pieces not bundled together.

lost or not lost   term which may be used in contracts of carriage in which the freight is prepaid: often, freight is not returnable whether the ship and/or the cargo are lost or not once having commenced the voyage. Many charter-parties provide that brokerage commission is payable whether the ship is lost or not.

low loader   trailer used for the movement of exceptionally large and heavy pieces of cargo.

lower hold   area of a ship's hold underneath the tween deck.

lower tween deck   space for carrying cargo above the lower hold of a ship and below the deck which divides the upper hold.

loyalty contract   contract between a liner conference and a shipper in which the shipper undertakes to ship his cargoes in the ships of member lines of that conference in return for a level of service and a discount, known as a contractor's rebate, or a special freight rate.

l.p.g.   liquid petroleum gas or liquefied petroleum gas.

l.s. & d.   *see* **landing, storage and delivery.**

l.t.   (1) *see* **long ton.**

l.t. (2) *see* **liner terms.**

luffing crane crane whose jib can be moved at different angles to the horizontal.

lump sum charter voyage charter for which the freight is payable as a lump sum rather than per tonne or other unit of cargo. The shipowner guarantees to lift a certain quantity of cargo but the charterer pays the same amount for freight irrespective of the quantity loaded.

l.w. low water.

l.w.o.n.t. low water ordinary neap tides.

l.w.o.s.t. low water ordinary spring tides.

M

m. (1) metre.

m. (2) *see* **measure.**

magnet device used for lifting scrap iron.

maiden voyage first voyage of a ship.

main deck deck of a ship from which the freeboard is determined.

main port port which handles a significant proportion of a country's sea-borne trade. It is normally one which can accommodate a large number of ships and which has a wide range of facilities. For liner ships, it is a port called at regularly.

maintain class (to) said of a ship, to pass the surveys which are carried out periodically by the ship's classification society to determine whether she is fit to continue trading according to the society's rules.

make good as general average (to) to compensate a cargo owner for loss or damage to cargo caused by a general average sacrifice.

manifest document containing a full list of a ship's cargo, extracted from the bills of lading. A copy, known as the **outward manifest**, is lodged with the Customs authorities at the port of loading. A further copy, known as the **inward manifest**, is similarly lodged at the discharge port, with one copy going to the ship's agent so that the unloading of the ship may be planned in advance.

maritime declaration of health statement signed by the master of a ship that health conditions on board his ship are good. This statement is submitted on arrival at a port to the health authorities who will then grant free pratique.

maritime lien claim against a ship enforced by means of her seizure, arising from non-payment of, for example, salvage charges or costs in relation to a collision.

marks and numbers markings distinctly displayed on goods being shipped, or on their packaging, for ease of identification. These include the port or place of destination and a package number, if there is more than one.

master commander of a merchant ship.

master foreign-going person who is officially qualified to command a foreign-going ship.

master's certificate official qualification enabling a person to command a merchant ship.

mate's receipt receipt, made out by the first officer, stating the quantity and condition of goods loaded on board the ship. This document is given to the shipper and later exchanged for the bill of lading.

Mauritanore voyage charter-party, published by the Baltic and International Maritime Conference (B.I.M.C.O.), used for shipments of iron ore from Mauritania. The full name of this charter-party is the General Ore Charter-party Mauritanian Terms.

max. maximum.

m.d.o. marine diesel oil.

mean draught average of the draughts forward and aft of a ship.

measure *or* **measurement** size of a piece of cargo or a consignment

89

expressed in cubic metres or cubic feet, determined by taking the (often extreme) length, width and height of the piece or consignment.

on the measurement   said of a freight rate which is payable on the basis of the cubic measurement of a cargo, generally per cubic metre.

measurement (of a ship)   calculation of a ship's register tonnage.

measurement cargo   cargo one tonne of which measures more than one cubic metre. Freight for measurement cargo is normally payable on the basis of its cubic measurement, that is, per cubic metre.

measurement rated cargo   cargo whose freight is payable on the basis of its cubic measurement, by means of a rate per cubic metre. Measurement rated cargoes are generally those which measure more than one cubic metre to one tonne.

measurement rules   rules of a liner conference concerning the method of determining the cubic measurement of a piece of cargo or a consignment consisting of more than one piece. Generally, a measurement is based on the extreme length, width and height of each piece or package with provisions for cargoes shipped in, for example, bags or drums.

mechanical ventilation   system of ventilating the holds of a ship whereby ventilators on deck are closed off and air is circulated mechanically through the holds, being dried, if necessary, by dehumidifying equipment. This method of ventilating is useful when the outside air contains a high level of humidity which would cause condensation damage to the cargo if introduced into the holds. This system is also known as **forced ventilation**.

Medcon   voyage charter-party used for shipments of coal from the East coast of the United Kingdom. It was devised by the Chamber of Shipping of the United Kingdom.

member line   shipping line which is a member of a liner conference and subject to the terms of membership which include charging its shippers only those freight rates agreed by the conference, loading and discharging only at those ports allocated by the conference to each line and, in the case of some conferences, pooling of cargoes and revenues amongst the lines.

memorandum of agreement   written contract for the purchase of a ship. It contains a description of the ship, the names of the parties, the purchase price and terms of payment, the date and place of delivery of the ship to the purchaser and all the other terms and conditions of the contract.

merchant   term often used in liner bills of lading to describe, as the case may be, the shipper, receiver or consignee, bill of lading holder or the agent of any of these.

merchant haulage   inland transport of shipping containers provided by the shipper or receiver of goods rather than by the ocean carrier.

merchant marine   all the ships of a country engaged in the carriage of goods.

Merseycon   voyage charter-party used for shipments of coal from the Mersey area of the United Kingdom. It was devised by the Chamber of Shipping of the United Kingdom.

metacentre   point where a vertical line passing through a ship's centre of buoyancy when she is upright meets a vertical line passing through her new centre of buoyancy when she is heeling.

metacentric height   distance between a ship's centre of gravity and her metacentre. The distance is critical since, if it is too small, the ship becomes unstable having a tendency to roll slowly. Such a ship is said to be tender. If the metacentric height is too large, the ship tends to roll quickly. In this case, she is said to be stiff. The metacentric height is known as the **g.m.** where g is the centre of gravity and m is the metacentre.

methane carrier   ship designed to carry methane (natural gas) in liquid form. This state is maintained by refrigeration.

metric ton   1,000 kilogrammes.

m.h.w.n.   mean high water neaps.

m.h.w.s.   mean high water springs.

min.   minimum.

min/max   minimum/maximum. When qualifying the contractual quantity in a voyage charter, this term signifies that freight is payable on that precise quantity, no more and no less.

misdeliver (to)   said of a carrier, to deliver cargo to the wrong consignee.

misdelivery   delivery of cargo by the carrier to the wrong consignee.

misdescribe (to)   to provide incorrect information, as a shipowner, concerning a ship or, as a shipper or charterer, concerning a cargo. *For further definition, see* **misdescription** *below.*

misdescription   incorrect information concerning a ship given by a shipowner to a charterer or concerning cargo given by a charterer or shipper to a shipowner or shipping line. This may give rise to a claim for extra costs or damages or, in some cases, cancellation of the contract of carriage.

miss the cancelling date (to)   said of a ship, to fail to be available to the charterer at the agreed place by the last date, known as the cancelling date, stipulated in the contract. This may give the charterer the right to cancel the charter.

mixed cargo   two or more products carried on board one ship.

mixing of cargo   placing of goods, for example in a ship, in such a way that they require sorting before being delivered.

m.l.w.n.   mean low water neaps.

m.l.w.s.   mean low water springs.

mobile crane   general purpose crane capable of being moved around a port. Some types are capable of lifting unusually heavy loads.

mol.   more or less.

molchop   *see* **more or less in charterer's option**.

mole   masonry structure projecting outwards from the shore, designed to protect the entrance to a port.

moloo.   *see* **more or less in owner's option**.

moor (to)   to attach a ship to the shore by means of ropes.

more in dispute if on board to be delivered   notation appearing on a bill of lading when the shipper is in disagreement with the ship as to the number of pieces or packages tallied on board.

more or less in charterer's option   option allowed to a voyage charterer to load up to a certain quantity, normally expressed as a percentage or a number of tonnes, over or under a quantity specified in the contract of carriage. This option may be sought if the charterer is not certain of the exact quantity which will be available at the time of loading.

more or less in owner's option   option allowed to a shipowner to carry up to a certain quantity, normally expressed as a percentage or a number of tonnes, over or under a quantity specified in the voyage charter. This option may be sought if the shipowner is not certain what the ship's cargo capacity will be, taking into consideration bunkers, stores and fresh water, or if he wants flexibility to adjust the ship's trim.

mother ship   ship which performs the main ocean leg of a voyage, being fed by smaller ships or barges. In particular, this term is used when referring to a barge-carrying ship.

moulded breadth   maximum breadth of a ship measured from the insides of her plating.

moulded depth   vertical distance from the keel to the uppermost deck, taken inside the ship's plating.

m/r   *see* **mate's receipt.**

m.s.   motor ship.

mt.   empty. This abbreviation is most often used to refer to shipping containers.

m.t.   *see* **metric ton.**

multideck ship   ship with several decks or levels, most suited to carrying general cargo.

multipurpose ship   any ship capable of carrying different types of cargo which require different methods of handling. There are several types of ship falling into this category, for example, ships which can carry roll-on roll-off cargo together with containers.

Murmapatit   voyage charter-party, published by the Shipchartering Coordinating Bureau, Moscow, used for shipments of apatite ore and apatite concentrates from Murmansk.

Murmapatitbill   bill of lading intended to be used for shipments of apatite ore and apatite concentrates from Murmansk under the Murmapatit charter-party.

m.v.   motor vessel.

N

n.a.a.b.s.a.   *see* **not always afloat but safe aground.**

Nanyozai   voyage charter-party, published by the Japan Shipping Exchange, used for shipments of logs.

narrow the laycan (to)   to reduce the number of days between the first of the laydays and the last. A shipowner may offer his ship to a prospective charterer with a large spread of dates in order to minimize the risk of the ship arriving after the cancelling date which may give the charterer the option of cancelling the charter. The prospective charterer may ask the shipowner to narrow the laycan because of berth or labour availability or because of cargo delivery requirements.

nautical mile   distance equal to 6,080 feet.

neap tide   tide whose range between high and low water is at its lowest.

neaped   said of a ship which is unable to leave a port or place because of a neap tide.

negligence clause   clause in a bill of lading or charter-party which seeks to relieve the shipowner or carrier of liability for losses caused by the negligence of his servants or agents.

net register tonnage *or* **net registered tonnage**   *see* **net tonnage.**

net terms   type of voyage charter in which cargo interests pay for loading and discharging.

net ton   ton of 2,000 lbs. Also referred to as a **short ton**.

net tonnage   the total of all enclosed spaces within a ship available for cargo, expressed in tons each of which is equivalent to one hundred cubic feet. Also referred to as **net register tonnage** or **net registered tonnage**.

net weight   weight of the goods only, not including their packing.

New Jason clause   protective clause inserted into a charter-party or bill of lading which provides that the shipowner is entitled to recover in general average even when the loss is caused by negligent navigation. The need for such a clause arises from the decision of an American court that, while American law exempted a shipowner from liability for loss or damage to cargo resulting from negligent navigation, this did not entitle the shipowner to recover in general average for such a loss.

New York Produce Exchange charter-party   form of time charter-party approved by the New York Produce Exchange.

newbuilding   ship which has been newly built. Until named, the ship is normally referred to by a (ship)yard number.

Nippon Kaiji Kyokai   Japanese ship classification society. *For the functions of a ship classification society, see* **classification society**.

Nipponore   voyage charter-party, published by the Japan Shipping Exchange, used for shipments of ore.

N.K.K.   Nippon Kaiji Kyokai—Japanese ship classification society. *See also* **classification society**.

no cure no pay   provision in a salvage agreement that salvage money is not payable unless the property is salved in accordance with that agreement.

n.o.e.   *see* **not otherwise enumerated**.

nomenclature   system of naming as, for example, the Brussels Tariff Nomenclature, a classification of all commodities carried internationally.

nominate a ship (to)   to designate a specific ship for a particular voyage.
   to be nominated   said in respect of a voyage for which a specific ship has yet to be designated by the shipowner or shipping line.

nomination   designation of a specific ship for a particular voyage by a shipowner or shipping line.

95

non-conference line   shipping line which operates on a route served by a liner conference but which is not a member of that conference. Also referred to as an **independent line** or an **outsider**.

non-contractor   person or company not having a loyalty contract with a particular liner conference and not, therefore, entitled to a contractor's rebate on the freight.

non-delivery   shortage of cargo at its destination.

non-hygroscopic cargo   cargo which does not absorb moisture, for example, from the atmosphere and does not suffer a change of weight during an ocean passage. It does, however, offer condensing surfaces and is therefore susceptible to damage from condensation.

non-negotiable bill of lading   bill of lading which is not a signed, original bill of lading and which is therefore not capable of being used to transfer title in the goods described in it.

non-reversible laytime   term used in a voyage charter-party to signify that the time allowed to the charterer for loading is to be treated separately from the time allowed for discharging for the purpose of calculating demurrage or despatch.

non-shipment   failure of goods to be loaded on board a particular ship.

non-vessel owning common carrier *or* **non-vessel operating common carrier**   person or company, often a forwarding agent, who does not own or operate the carrying ship but who contracts with a shipping line for the carriage of the goods of third parties to whom he normally issues a house bill of lading.

n.o.r.   *see* **notice of readiness**.

Norgrain   voyage charter-party used for shipments of grain from the United States of America and from Canada. Its full name is the North American Grain Charterparty and it is issued by the Association of Ship Brokers and Agents (U.S.A.).

n.o.s.   not otherwise specified. *For definition, see* **not otherwise enumerated**.

not always afloat but safe aground   provision in a charter-party that the charterer has the right to order the ship to a port where she may touch the bottom in safety.

not otherwise enumerated   category in the freight tariff of a shipping line or liner conference which covers commodities not specifically described elsewhere in the tariff. Also referred to as **not otherwise specified**.

not otherwise specified   *see* **not otherwise enumerated**.

note protest (to)   as master of a ship, to make a declaration before a notary public on arrival in port that the ship has encountered circumstances beyond his control, such as heavy weather, which may have caused damage to the ship or her cargo. It may be necessary for the master to make this declaration, for example, to avoid liability for damage to cargo.

notice of readiness   provision in a voyage charter that the shipowner or master must advise the charterer when the ship has arrived and is ready to load or discharge for laytime to start counting. The clause containing this provision often stipulates the particular hours and days when this notice may be tendered and how soon afterwards laytime commences.

notice of redelivery   written notice given by the time charterer to the shipowner giving the date when the ship is to be returned to the shipowner at the end of the period of the charter. Charter-parties often stipulate that several such notices be given at agreed intervals as the date of redelivery approaches.

notify party   party, whose name and address appear in a bill of lading, who is to be notified by the shipping company or its agent of the arrival of the goods at the discharge port. The notify party is often an agent for the receiver of the goods who arranges for their clearance and transport to the receiver's premises. There is normally a box on the bill of lading into which the details of the notify party are inserted.

n.r.t.   net register tonnage or net registered tonnage. *For definition, see* **net tonnage**.

Nubaltwood   (1) voyage charter-party, published by the Chamber of Shipping of the United Kingdom, used for shipments of timber from the Baltic and Norway to the United Kingdom and the Republic of Ireland.

Nubaltwood   (2) bill of lading intended to be used for shipments of timber from the Baltic and Norway to the United Kingdom and the Republic of Ireland under the Nubaltwood charter-party.

Nuvoy   general purpose voyage charter-party, published by the British Chamber of Foreign Trade.

Nuvoybill   bill of lading intended to be used for shipments under the Nuvoy charter-party.

n.v.o.c.   non-vessel owning carrier.

n.v.o.c.c.   *see* **non-vessel owning common carrier.**

N.Y.P.E. (c/p)   *see* **New York Produce Exchange charter-party.**

O

o.b.o.   *see* **ore/bulk/oil carrier.**

ocean waybill   document, issued by a shipping line to a shipper, which serves as a receipt for the goods and evidence of the contract of carriage. In these respects it resembles a bill of lading but, unlike a bill of lading, it is not a document of title; it bears the name of the consignee who has only to identify himself in order to take delivery of the cargo. Because it is not negotiable, the ocean waybill is not acceptable to banks as collateral security. The purpose of the ocean waybill is to avoid the delays to ships and cargoes which occur when bills of lading are late in arriving at the discharge port. This document is also referred to as a **liner waybill** or a **sea waybill** or simply a **waybill.**

off hire   said of a ship on time charter for which hire money has temporarily ceased to be paid by the charterer, for example, because of a breakdown of the ship or her equipment.

off hire survey   inspection carried out at the time a ship is redelivered by a time charterer to a shipowner at the end of the period of the charter. The inspection is carried out to determine whether the ship is in the same condition, wear and tear excepted, as on delivery. The quantity of bunkers is ascertained for comparison with the amounts specified in the charter-party. By agreement, the ship is inspected by one surveyor only or one surveyor for each of the two parties. Which party pays for the survey and whether the time taken counts for the purpose of calculating hire money are agreed in the charter-party.

offer firm (to)   to make an offer which is not conditional in any way and is binding on the party making it, provided that it is accepted in full and within any time limit specified in it.

official number   number allocated to a ship by the authorities of a country when the ship is registered, for the purpose of identification.

oil barge   river barge designed for the carriage of oil cargoes.

oil port   port whose main or only type of cargo handled is oil, often with deep water jetties to accommodate large oil tankers and with storage tanks and refineries.

oil tanker   ship designed for the carriage of oil in bulk, her cargo space consisting of several, or indeed many, tanks. Size and capacity range from the ultra large crude carrier (u.l.c.c.) of over half a million tonnes deadweight to the small coastal tanker. Tankers load their cargo by gravity from the shore or by shore pumps and discharge using their own pumps.

oil/bulk/ore carrier   *see* **ore/bulk/oil carrier** *below*.

on hire survey   inspection carried out at the time a ship is delivered by a shipowner to a time charterer at the beginning of the period of the charter. This inspection is carried out to determine the condition of the ship which may subsequently be compared with her condition at the end of the charter. The quantity of bunkers is ascertained for comparison with the amounts specified in the charter-party. By agreement, the ship is inspected by one surveyor only or one surveyor for each of the two parties. Which party pays for the survey and whether the time taken counts for the purpose of calculating hire money are agreed in the charter-party.

on-carriage   carriage of cargo beyond the port or place where it is discharged from a sea-going or ocean-going ship, by another means of transport such as truck, train or barge. This movement is often sub-contracted by the ocean carrier to another company and it is important for the shipper or receiver to determine which carrier is responsible for any loss or damage.

on-carrier   person or company who contracts to transport cargo from the port or place of discharge of a sea-going or ocean-going ship to another, often inland, destination by a different means of transport such as truck, train or barge.

on-carry (to)   to carry cargo from the port or place of discharge of a sea-going or ocean-going ship to another, often inland, destination by a different means of transport such as truck, train or barge.

one safe berth   *see* **safe berth**.

one safe port *see* **safe port.**

on-forwarding the arranging of on-carriage of goods beyond the port of discharge of a ship to their final destination.

o.o. in owner's option *See under* **owner.**

o/o *see* **ore/oil carrier.**

open said of a ship which is available as from a specified date at a particular place to steam to another port, if necessary, to load her next cargo, having discharged the last one.

open conference liner conference which does not require its member lines to vote on the admission of a new member. *See also* **conference.**

open rate freight rate negotiated by a shipper or freight forwarder with a shipping line or liner conference for shipping in excess of a minimum agreed quantity of cargo on any one ship. It is lower than the published tariff rate and generally applies to shipments of one commodity from one port of loading to one port of discharging.

open rated cargo cargo which is the subject of an open rate. *See also* **open rate** *above.*

open roadstead expanse of water situated off a port where ships are able to anchor safely but which is not sheltered.

open shelter-deck ship *or* **open shelter-decker** shelter-deck ship whose tonnage opening is kept permanently open. This type of ship was designed such that her registered tonnage would not include the shelter-deck space although this space is capable of carrying cargo. *See also* **shelter-deck ship.**

open side container shipping container with side doors which drop down to give unrestricted access to the sides of the container for loading or discharging. When provided by an ocean carrier, this type of container is sometimes the subject of an additional charge on the freight rate.

open top container shipping container which has an open top instead of a solid roof to enable cargo, such as timber or scrap metal, to be loaded from the top. The container is covered by waterproof sheeting while in transit. When provided by an ocean carrier, this type of container is sometimes the subject of an additional charge on the freight rate.

open/closed shelter-deck ship *or* **open/closed shelter-decker** shelter-deck ship whose tonnage opening may be left open or converted to a fully enclosed tween decker depending on the trade in which she is engaged. *See also* **shelter-deck ship**.

opening of navigation date when an area or waterway is opened to shipping. This follows a period when navigation is prohibited, often because of severe ice conditions during winter.

operate a ship (to) to run a ship. There are two principal aspects of operating a ship: technical and commercial. Technical operation includes crewing and supplying the ship, keeping her machinery and equipment in working order and stowing cargoes safely and efficiently. Commercial operation is concerned more with booking cargoes, negotiating freight rates and bunker prices and appointing ship's agents at the ports of call.

optional cargo cargo which is destined for one of the ship's discharge ports, the exact one not being known when the goods are loaded. It must therefore be stowed in such a position that it can be removed at any of the optional ports without disturbing other cargo.

orders set of instructions given or sent by the shipowner or ship operator to the master of a ship concerning the next voyage. These instructions include the names of the intended ports of loading, bunkering and discharging together with the names, addresses, telephone numbers and cable addresses of the ship's agents at each port, details of the cargo, a schedule of bunkers needed for the voyage and the required notices of expected arrival. When the next voyage is not known, a ship is said to be **awaiting orders** and the master may be instructed to anchor where he is or to steam in the direction of the area where the shipowner expects to find a cargo.

ore carrier large ship, generally gearless and with large hatchways, designed to be used for the carriage of various types of ore. Because of the high density of ore, ore carriers have a relatively high centre of gravity to prevent them being stiff when at sea, that is, rolling heavily with possible stress to the hull.

ore/bulk/oil carrier large multi-purpose ship designed to carry cargoes either of ore or other bulk commodities or oil so as to reduce the time the ship would be in ballast if restricted to one type of commodity. The cargo is loaded into central holds and, if oil, into side tanks as well. This type of ship is sometimes referred to as a **bulk/oil carrier**.

Orecon voyage charter-party, published by the Baltic and International

Maritime Conference (B.I.M.C.O.), used for shipments of ore from Scandinavia to Poland.

ore/oil carrier   ship designed to carry either ore or oil in bulk, the purpose being to reduce the time the ship would spend in ballast. Ore is carried only in the central holds whereas oil is carried in wing tanks and in the central holds as well, if required.

original bill of lading   bill of lading which bears the original signature of the master of a ship or his agent. It is exchanged for the goods at the place of destination of the contract of carriage. *See also* **bill of lading**.

o.s.b.   one safe berth. *See* **safe berth**.

o.s.d.   *see* **open shelter-deck ship**.

o.s. & d. report *or* **o.s.d. report**   over, short and damage report. *For definition, see* **outturn report**.

o.s.p.   one safe port. *See* **safe port**.

o/t   *see* **overtime**.

out of gauge   said of cargo whose dimensions exceed any of the external dimensions of the container in which, or on which, it is carried.

outport   port which is served infrequently or by transhipment by a shipping line or by the member lines of a liner conference. The freight to such ports sometimes attracts a surcharge known as an **outport additional**.

outreach   maximum distance to which loading or discharging equipment can extend outwards. There are various points from which this distance may be measured, for example, from the quay wall or fendering, or the landside end of the jib of a shore crane. Also known as the **reach**.

outsider   shipping line which operates on a route served by a liner conference but which is not a member of that conference. Also referred to as a **non-conference line** or an **independent line**.

outturn (to)   said of cargo, to be discharged from a ship. This term is normally qualified by the condition or quantity of the cargo, that is, whether it is damaged or whether the quantity is greater or less than the quantity on the ship's manifest.

outturn report   written statement by a stevedoring company in which the condition of cargo discharged from a ship is noted along with any discrepancies in the quantity compared with the ship's manifest. Also referred to as an **over, short and damage report**.

outturn weight   weight of a cargo ascertained when it is discharged from a ship. Freight on bulk cargoes is sometimes payable on the basis of this weight.

outward   term relating to the departure of a ship from a port. For example, an outward cargo is one which has been loaded at the port in question and destined for another port. A ship's outward charges are those incurred in leaving a port, such as outward pilotage.

over, short and damage report   *see* **outturn report**.

overage   cargo discharged in excess of the quantity on the ship's manifest.

overcarriage   the carriage of cargo beyond the port for which it was intended.

overcarry (to)   to carry cargo beyond the port for which it was intended.

over-consumption   the use of too great an amount of fuel per day over a period of time by a ship. If the ship is on time charter and the charter-party contains a guaranteed maximum daily consumption, over-consumption would give rise to a claim by the time charterer against the shipowner for the excess cost of bunkers.

overlanded cargo *or* **overlanding**   cargo which has been discharged at a port for which it was not intended according to the ship's manifest. The ship's agent, on behalf of the shipowner or carrier, tries, by means of the shipping marks on the cargo and by contacting the ship's agents at the other discharge ports on the ship's itinerary, to identify the correct destination. In many instances, cargo which cannot be identified and disposed of within a certain period of time may be auctioned by the port authority.

overload (to)   to load a ship or vehicle with goods whose weight is in excess of that which the ship or vehicle is permitted by law to carry.

overside discharge   the removal of goods from a ship directly on to barges using the ship's cranes or derricks. When instructed to deliver cargo in this way, shipping lines often insert a clause in the bill of lading to the effect that this will be carried out provided that sufficient barges are available. This is to ensure that there is no delay in the discharging of the ship.

overstow (to)   to stow one item of cargo on top of another in a ship. It is important for a cargo superintendent to know whether a particular product may be overstowed by another, or at all, taking into consideration the safety of the cargo and of the ship when at sea.

overtime   period outside normal working hours when work, if required, is available at an extra cost. It is often agreed in charter-parties that the cost of overtime is payable by the party who orders it.

overtonnaging   situation where there are too many ships generally, or in a particular trade, for the level of available cargoes.

owner   widely used short form for shipowner.
   in owner's option   term in a charter-party which stipulates that the shipowner has a choice in specific circumstances. For example, in a voyage charter, the owner may have the option of specifying the exact quantity of cargo to be loaded.

owner's agents   ship's agent nominated by, and paid by, the shipowner in accordance with the charter-party.

owner's broker   shipbroker who acts on behalf of a shipowner in the negotiations leading to the chartering out of that owner's ship.

P

package limitation   maximum amount of money per package for which a carrier may be liable under the contract of carriage in the event of loss or damage to cargo. This amount is determined by agreement of the parties or by law.

packing list   document detailing the contents of a case or crate, or itemizing a consignment.

pallet   flat tray, generally made of wood but occasionally of steel, on which goods, particularly those in boxes, cartons or bags, can be stacked. Its purpose is to facilitate the movement of such goods, mainly by the use of fork-lift trucks.

pallet rules   rules of a liner conference governing cargoes shipped on pallets. These rules include the method of assessing freight, the conference's requirements as to the nature of the pallet and the way in which goods should be packed on it and secured to it.

palletized   said of goods loaded on to pallets.   *See also* **pallet** *above.*

Panamax   largest size of ship capable of transiting the Panama Canal.

pandi club *or* **p. & i. club**   *see* **protection and indemnity club.**

Panstone   voyage charter-party, published by the Chamber of Shipping of the United Kingdom, used for shipments of stone.

paragraph ship   cargo-carrying ship so called because the regulations of various countries concerning the construction, equipment and manning of ships contain separate sections, or paragraphs, for ships of different gross tonnages. A paragraph ship is a ship whose gross tonnage is just below a certain figure which, if it had been exceeded, would have entailed more stringent requirements and a higher running cost.

paramount clause   clause in a bill of lading or charter-party which stipulates that the contract of carriage is governed by the Hague Rules or the Hague-Visby Rules or the enactment of these rules in the country having jurisdiction over the contract.

parcel   (1) a package.

parcel   (2) a complete consignment.

parcel tanker   tanker designed to carry several grades of liquid cargo including chemicals and refined oil products.

part cargo   goods which do not represent the entire cargo for a particular ship but whose quantity is sufficient to be carried on charter terms.

part charter   the chartering of a ship to carry a quantity of goods which represents only a part of the cargo.

particular average   marine insurance term denoting a partial loss.

peak tank   small tank situated at the extreme forward end (fore peak tank) or after end (after peak tank) of a ship. It normally holds water ballast and is used to help to trim the ship, that is, to adjust the draughts forward and aft.

performance claim claim made by a time charterer against a shipowner when the ship has been unable to achieve the speed agreed in the charter-party or has consumed too much fuel or both.

performance clause clause in a time charter-party which stipulates that, should the ship be unable to achieve the agreed speed or should she consume too much fuel, the charterer is entitled to recover from the shipowner the cost of time lost and the extra fuel, normally by means of a deduction from hire money.

perishable goods goods, notably foodstuffs, which are liable to decay if the conditions within the ship or shipping container in which they are being carried are not strictly controlled or, in some cases, if the voyage time is unduly extended. Perishable goods require either refrigeration or ventilation or both.

permanent dunnage strips of timber fixed to the frames of a ship, often horizontally but sometimes vertically, to keep cargo away from the sides of the ship, to avoid both damage and condensation. Also known as **cargo battens** and **spar ceiling**.

p.f.t. per freight ton. *For definition, see* **freight ton**.

p. & i. bunker deviation clause clause in a charter-party giving the shipowner the right to deviate from the contracted route for the purpose of taking on fuel.

p. & i. club *see* **protection and indemnity club**.

piece weight weight of each piece or package of a consignment.

pier structure at which ships can berth, built at right angles to the shore.

pier to house said of a freight rate or service provided by a container shipping line whereby goods are received into the care of the line at the port terminal in the country of export and delivered to the consignee's premises.

pier to pier said of a freight rate or service provided by a container shipping line whereby goods are received into the care of the line at the port terminal in the country of export and delivered to the consignee at the port terminal in the country of destination.

pilferage petty theft.

pilot person who is qualified to assist the master of a ship to navigate when entering or leaving a port.

pilotage   the act, carried out by a pilot, of assisting the master of a ship in navigation when entering or leaving a port. Sometimes used to define the fee payable for the services of a pilot.

pilotage dues   fee payable by the owner or operator of a ship for the services of a pilot. This fee is normally based on the ship's tonnage.

pitch (to)   said of a ship, to rock lengthwise.

place a ship off hire (to)   as time charterer, to cease temporarily to pay hire money to the shipowner while, for example, the ship or her equipment are broken down.

plate clamp   device fixed to the edge of a steel plate to prevent it from slipping when being lifted.

platform flat   flat steel surface on to which awkward cargoes can be loaded for carriage in containerships. This flat has no ends or sides. When these flats are empty, several may be interlocked in a stack which has the same dimensions as a standard container enabling them to be transported in the same way. When provided by an ocean carrier, this type of conveyance is often the subject of an additional charge on the freight rate.

Plimsoll line   summer load line of a ship, that is, the line painted on the sides of a ship which shows the maximum depth to which the ship's hull may be immersed when in a summer zone. The line is marked with an S. Also referred to as **summer marks**. *See also* **load line zone**.

p.l.t.c.   *see* **port liner term charges**.

point to port rate   freight rate which includes all costs from an inland place in the exporting country to the port of discharge in the importing country.

Polcoalbill   bill of lading intended to be used for shipments of coal under the Polcoalvoy charter-party.

Polcoalvoy   voyage charter-party, published by the Baltic and International Maritime Conference (B.I.M.C.O.), used for shipments of coal.

pontoon   flat-bottomed vessel with a shallow draught.

pontoon hatch cover   large steel slab used to cover a hatchway and lifted on and off by a crane.

pooling   sharing of cargo or the profit or loss from freight by member lines of a liner conference. Pooling arrangements do not exist in all conferences.

port   (1) harbour having facilities for ships to moor and load or discharge.

port   (2) left side of a ship when facing towards the front or forward end.

port dues   charge levied against a shipowner or ship operator by a port authority for the use of a port.

port liner term charges   cargo handling charges levied on the shipper by the shipping line at the port of loading.

port log   statement, prepared by the ship's agent at the loading and discharging ports, which shows the dates and times of arrival of the ship and the commencement and completion of loading and discharging. It details the quantity of cargo loaded or discharged each day, the hours worked and the hours stopped with the reasons for the stoppages, such as bad weather, a strike or breakdown of equipment. Also referred to as a **statement of facts**.

port mark   the name of the discharge port marked on goods or their packaging to help prevent them being discharged at the wrong port or, if they are, to enable them to be rerouted.

port of refuge   port, not on a ship's itinerary, which she calls at because of some unforeseen hazard at sea and where she may undergo repairs, refuel or resecure cargo to enable her to continue the voyage.

port of registry   place where a ship is registered with the authorities, thus establishing her nationality. The name of the port is marked on the stern of the ship.

port to point rate   freight rate which includes all costs from the port of loading in the exporting country to an inland place in the importing country.

portal crane   crane which is raised from the ground and often on rails to permit movement along the quay.

position containers (to)   to bring empty shipping containers to a location or area where they will next be loaded.

possessory lien   the right of a shipowner to retain cargo until the freight or any general average contribution is paid.

post fixture   work carried out by a shipowner or shipbroker after the negotiations for the charter of a ship have been concluded. This includes payment of hire or freight, calculation of despatch or demurrage and the resolution of any disputes.

post-entry   declaration to the Customs authorities after clearance of imported or exported goods amending details on the original entry.

p.p.   (1) picked ports.

p.p.   (2) posted price—the currently available price of a particular grade of oil.

pratique   permission granted by the authorities at a port, being satisfied as to the state of health of those on board a ship on arrival, for them to make physical contact with the shore. Also referred to as **free pratique**. A ship which is the subject of such permission is said to be **in free pratique**.

preamble   first few lines of a charter-party in which the parties to the contract and the ship are identified.

pre-entry   presentation to the Customs authorities of export or import declarations prior to the clearance of the goods.

pre-shipment charges   any charges incurred prior to the shipment of a cargo which are not included in the sea freight.

pre-sling (to)   to place goods in slings which are left in position and used for the loading to, and discharging from, a ship. This is a form of unit load the purpose of which is to simplify handling and increase the rate of loading and discharging. Pre-slinging is used for products which cannot be palletized or containerized. It is a requirement of some importing countries for certain products.

pre-stow (to)   to decide in advance the stowage of a cargo on a ship.

private form   standard charter-party devised and used by a particular company. The majority of these charter-parties are used by oil companies when chartering tankers.

pro forma charter-party   document containing all the terms and conditions of a contract between a shipowner and a charterer but which is unsigned and therefore is not the contract itself.

pro forma disbursements account   statement sent by a ship's agent at a port to the shipowner in advance of the ship's call at the port. It consists of the expenses which are likely to be incurred, including port charges, pilotage, towage and the agent's commission. This account is used to help the shipowner estimate the viability of a voyage and serves as a request by the agent for sufficient funds to be made available prior to the ship's arrival.

product carrier   small tanker used to carry refined oil products from the refinery to the consumer.

promotional rate   concessionary freight rate offered to a shipper by a shipping line or liner conference to facilitate the sale of goods into a new market.

propane carrier   ship designed to carry propane in liquid form. The propane is carried in tanks within the holds; it remains in liquid form by means of pressure and refrigeration. Such ships are also suitable for the carriage of butane.

prospects   expectations. This term is used most often to denote the expectations of completion of loading or discharging of a cargo although it can also mean any expectations, for example, the prospects of getting a berth or obtaining a certain number of gangs.

protecting agent   person or company appointed by a shipowner to protect his interests and to supervise the work carried out by the ship's agent when the owner's ship is in port. The ship's agent may be the only agent at the port or he may have been appointed or nominated by the charterer and therefore not the choice of the shipowner. Also referred to as a **supervisory agent** or **protective agent**.

protecting clauses   *see* **protective clauses** *below.*

protection and indemnity club *or* **protection and indemnity association**   association of shipowners who, by means of contributions, known as calls, provide mutual protection against liabilities not covered by insurance, such as claims for injury to crew and loss or damage to cargo.

protective agent   *see* **protecting agent** *above.*

protective clauses   clauses in a charter-party which provide contingencies for unforeseen situations, such as ice, strikes, general average or collision. Also known as **protecting clauses**.

110

protest   declaration, made before a notary public by the master of a ship on arrival in port, that the ship has encountered circumstances beyond his control, such as heavy weather, which may have caused damage to the ship or her cargo. This declaration may be necessary, for example, to avoid liability for damage to cargo.

pumpman   rating who tends to the pumps of a tanker.

purposes   time allowed in a voyage charter-party for loading and discharging combined, expressed as a number of days or hours. Also referred to as **all purposes**.

pusher   river tug which moves barges by pushing rather than towing.

Q

quay   solid structure alongside a navigable waterway, used for the loading and discharging of ships.

quote (to)   as a charterer, to make known that a ship is sought for a particular cargo or, as a shipowner, to advertise the availability of his ship for charter. Most often this activity is carried out using the services of shipbrokers.

R

raised quarter-deck ship   ship whose upper deck is raised at the stern end in order to increase cargo capacity.

ramp   inclined plane which connects a roll-on roll-off ship to the shore or quay on which rolling cargo is wheeled or driven into or out of the ship. This ramp may be at the forward end (bow ramp), the after end (stern ramp) or the side (side ramp) of the ship and very often is designed to make a watertight door to cover the opening in the ship. Interior ramps also connect the different decks in a roll-on roll-off ship.

range of ports   series of ports normally on the same coast. Often a charter-party will contain a range of ports at which the ship may discharge, one of which is to be nominated by the charterer by a specific date. The range is generally expressed by means of the names of the ports at the two ends, for example the Antwerp–Hamburg range.

rate   frequently used term to mean rate of freight or freight rate. *For definition, see* **rate of freight** *below.*

rate of demurrage   amount payable by a voyage charterer to a shipowner for each day used to load and/or discharge cargo in excess of the time allowed in the charter-party.

rate of discharge *or* **rate of discharging**   number of tonnes of cargo discharged each day from a ship. Such a provision is often included in the terms of a voyage charter.

rate of freight   amount of money paid to a shipowner or shipping line for the carriage of each unit of cargo, such as a tonne, a cubic metre or container load. Also known as a **freight rate**.

rate of loading   number of tonnes of cargo loaded per day into a ship. Such a provision is often included in the terms of a voyage charter.

reach (of a crane)   maximum distance to which loading or discharging equipment can extend outwards. There are various points from which this distance may be measured, for example, from the quay wall or fendering, or the landside end of a jib of a shore crane. Also known as the **outreach**.

received for shipment bill of lading   bill of lading evidencing that the goods have been received into the care of the carrier, but not yet loaded on board. It also serves as evidence of the contract of carriage and is a document of title, although because the goods have not necessarily been loaded on to the ship, this type of bill of lading is not always acceptable to banks as collateral security.

receiver   party who receives the cargo at the place of destination in the contract of carriage.

receiving dates   two dates between which a liner ship receives cargo for loading. These dates are advertised by the shipping line or its agents.

recharter (to)   said of a charterer of a ship, to charter or hire the ship out to another party. Also referred to as **to sub-let** and **to sub-charter**.

recovery agent   person or company whose business is to recover as much as

112

possible, from the responsible parties, of the money paid by insurance under-writers to cargo interests for loss or damage to cargo. Any money recovered is passed to the underwriters and the agent is paid a fee for his services, often a percentage of the amount recovered.

redeliver (to)   as time charterer, to return a ship to the shipowner at the end of the period of the charter.

redelivery   return of a ship by the time charterer to the shipowner at the end of the period of the charter.

redelivery certificate   document, signed by or on behalf of the shipowner and the charterer, certifying the time, date and place of redelivery of the ship, that is, the returning of the ship by the time charterer to the shipowner at the end of the period of the charter. The certificate also states the quantities of bunkers on board at the time of redelivery.

redly.   *see* **redelivery.**

Redwood Scale   scale which measures the viscosity of oils, for example, fuel oil and diesel oil, in seconds. The greater the number of seconds, the higher the viscosity of a grade of oil.

reefer box   *see* **refrigerated container.**

reefer ship   *see* **refrigerated ship.**

re-export (to)   to export goods from a country to which they have previously been imported, either in the same condition or after processing.

refrigerated container   insulated shipping container designed to carry car-goes requiring temperature control, such as dairy produce, meat, fish and fruit. It is fitted with a refrigeration unit which is connected to the carrying ship's electrical power supply. Also referred to as a **reefer box.**

refrigerated ship   ship designed to carry goods requiring refrigeration, such as meat and fruit. A refrigerated ship, or reefer ship as it is sometimes referred to, has insulated holds into which cold air is passed at the temperature appropriate to the goods being carried.

register (to)   (1) to record the ownership of a ship with the authorities of a country. *See also* **registration** (1) *below.*

register (to) (2) to record a ship's arrival with the port authority, usually at a port which is congested and where ships are allocated a berth in order of their arrival. *See also* **registration** (2) *below.*

register tonnage *or* **registered tonnage** volume of a ship expressed in tons each of which is equivalent to one hundred cubic feet.

registration (1) recording of the ownership of a ship with the authorities of a country. Details of the owner or owners are submitted, as are plans and details of the ship, including measurements and tonnages. The name of the ship and her port of registry must be painted on the ship. Registration of a ship provides her with a nationality and makes her subject to the laws of the country in which she is is registered.

registration (2) recording of a ship's arrival with the port authority, usually at a port which is congested and where ships are allocated a berth in order of their arrival. In ports where there is likely to be a prolonged delay before a berth becomes vacant, some ships, after registration, proceed to another port to discharge and return to take up their original place in the queue.

Registro Italiano Navale Italian ship classification society. *For the functions of a ship classification society, see* **classification society**.

release a bill of lading (to) to provide the shipper with an original bill of lading, often in exchange for the freight.

release cargo (to) as carrier, to relinquish control of a cargo at the place of destination.

remaining on board said of the quantity of cargo or bunkers still on board a ship at a particular point of a voyage, for example, on sailing from one of the ports on her itinerary.

remeasure a ship (to) to recalculate a ship's register tonnages when, for example, the rules of measurement are altered or it appears to the authorities of a country that the tonnages of a foreign ship differ substantially from those which would apply had the ship been measured in that country.

removable deck deck of a ship which is capable of being removed and stowed out of the way. This type of deck is found in some car carriers and is removed when the ship is carrying a bulk cargo.

reporting point place where a ship is required to report when passing, for example, to a port authority when approaching the port. Also referred to as a **calling-in-point**.

reposition containers (to)   to move empty shipping containers away from a location or area where there are no further loads to one where there are.

reserve buoyancy   volume of watertight space of a ship above the water-line, providing safety for the ship while at sea.

respondentia   the borrowing of money by a master of a ship using the cargo as security. Also called a **respondentia loan**. The document in which the cargo is pledged is known as a **respondentia bond**.

return cargo   cargo which enables a ship to return loaded to the port or area where her previous cargo was loaded.

return load   load which enables a vehicle to return loaded to the place or country from where its previous load came. Also referred to as a **back load**.

reversible laytime   term used in a voyage charter-party to signify that the time allowed for loading may, at the charterer's option, be added to the time allowed for discharging for the purpose of calculating demurrage or despatch.

R.I.   Registro Italiano Navale—Italian ship classification society. *For the functions of a ship classification society, see* **classification society**.

rigger   person who rigs a ship's derrick in readiness for hoisting cargo.

rigging screw   screw which applies tension to ropes or chains used for lashing cargo.

roads *or* **roadstead**   expanse of water situated off a port where ships are able to anchor safely.

r.o.b.   *see* **remaining on board**.

roll (to)   said of a ship, to rock sideways.

rolling cargo   cargo which is on wheels, such as trucks or trailers, and which can be driven or towed on to a ship.

roll-on roll-off   system of loading and discharging a ship whereby the cargo is driven on and off on ramps. A ship designed to handle cargo in this way is known as a **roll-on roll-off ship** or **ro-ro ship**.

ro-ro   *see* **roll-on roll-off** *above.*

rotation   sequence in which a ship calls at the ports on her itinerary.

round voyage   voyage involving two legs the second of which brings the ship back to the geographical area where the first leg commenced.

run aground (to)   said of a ship, to touch the bottom.

running days   consecutive calendar days of 24 hours including week-ends and holidays.

S

s.   summer.

safe aground   term in a charter-party which allows the charterer to order the ship to a port or place where she may safely touch the bottom. This term is often part of the expression **not always afloat but safe aground**.

safe berth   term in a charter-party which places the responsibility on to cargo interests to order the chartered ship to a berth which is physically safe for her while she is there for the purpose of loading or discharging.

safe port   term in a charter-party which places the responsibility on to cargo interests to order the chartered ship to a port which is physically and politically safe for her to reach, remain at and leave, taking into consideration the cargo to be loaded or discharged.

safe working load   maximum load which can safely be borne by a lifting or hauling appliance, such as a crane or winch. The safe working load is generally marked clearly on the equipment and should not be exceeded.

safety margin   allowance made for delays to a ship or for extra steaming time caused, for example, by bad weather, when calculating the quantity of bunkers required for a voyage.

safety radio-telegraphy certificate   document, issued by the authorities of a country, which certifies that a ship is equipped with suitable radio equipment taking into consideration her size, number of crewmen and the type of voyages which she is likely to undertake.

sag (to)   said of a ship, to be loaded in such a way that the centre of the ship is depressed below the level of the two ends. This bending of the ship's plating may result in damage or distortion.

said to contain   term in a bill of lading signifying that the master and carrier are unaware of the nature or quantity of the contents of a carton, crate or bundle and are relying on the description furnished by the shipper.

sail (to)   (1) to navigate.

sail (to)   (2) to depart from a port.

sailing schedule or sailing card   printed list of current and future sailings issued by a liner company. It contains the names of the ships, receiving and sailing dates against each of the loading ports and estimated arrival dates at the discharge ports. It also contains the names and telephone numbers of the line's agents for enquiries and bookings.

sale and purchase broker   person who negotiates the terms for the sale of a ship on behalf of buyer or seller.

Saleform   memorandum of agreement giving details of the purchase of a ship, devised by the Norwegian Shipbrokers' Association. *See also* **memorandum of agreement**.

salvage (charges)   remuneration paid to a person who saves a ship, her equipment or cargo from loss or damage at sea. The amount is assessed by a court of law according to the value of the salved property, the degree of danger to which it was exposed, the risks borne by the salvor and the degree of skill exercised in saving the property. All the parties contribute in proportion to the value of their salved property.

salvage (service)   action taken to save a ship, her equipment or cargo from loss or damage at sea.

salvage   property saved from loss or damage at sea.

salvage agreement   written agreement signed by the master or owner of a

117

salving ship and the master or owner of a ship in need of salvage assistance, containing their names, the amount of salvage payable and a provision that the service is provided on a no cure no pay basis, that is, that salvage is not payable unless the property is salved in accordance with the agreement.

Salvage Association organization, having a world-wide network of representatives, often appointed to carry out surveys when loss or damage has occurred to ships or cargoes overseas. The Association does not normally determine liability for a loss; it merely reports on the extent of the loss, the probable reasons for it and the likely cost of repairs.

salve (to) to save a ship, her equipment or cargo from loss or damage at sea.

salvor person performing a salvage operation.

Saturdays, Sundays and holidays excepted term in a charter-party which provides that Saturdays, Sundays and public holidays do not count in the calculation of laytime. *See also* **even if used** *and* **unless used.**

Saturdays, Sundays and holidays included term in a charter-party which provides that Saturdays, Sundays and public holidays count in the calculation of laytime, whether or not used for loading or discharging, as the case may be.

s.b. *see* **safe berth.**

s.b.m. single buoy mooring.

Scancon general purpose voyage charter-party, published by the Baltic and International Maritime Conference (B.I.M.C.O.), for use with Scandinavian charterers.

Scanconbill bill of lading intended to be used for shipments under the Scancon charter-party.

Scanorecon voyage charter-party, published by the Baltic and International Maritime Conference (B.I.M.C.O.), used for shipments of iron ore from Scandinavia.

Scanoreconbill bill of lading intended to be used for shipments of iron ore under the Scanorecon charter-party.

scantlings sizes of materials used in the construction of a ship.

118

scow   flat-bottomed lighter.

s.c.q.   *see* **special commodity quotation.**

s.e.   subject to enquiry.

sea waybill   document, issued by a shipping line to a shipper, which serves as a receipt for the goods and evidence of the contract of carriage. In these respects it resembles a bill of lading but, unlike a bill of lading, it is not a document of title; it bears the name of the consignee who has only to identify himself in order to take delivery of the cargo. Because it is not negotiable, the sea waybill is not acceptable to banks as collateral security. The purpose of the sea waybill is to avoid the delays to ships and cargoes which occur when bills of lading are late in arriving at the discharge port. The sea waybill is also referred to as a **liner waybill** or an **ocean waybill** or simply a **waybill.**

seal   security device attached to the doors of a shipping container such that, if it is intact on arrival at destination, this is proof that the container has not been opened while in transit.

seasonal tropical zone   one of several geographical areas, defined by the International Conference on Load Lines, where, during certain periods of the year which vary according to the particular zone, a ship's hull may be immersed no deeper than her tropical load line.

seasonal winter zone   one of several geographical areas, defined by the International Conference on Load Lines, where, during certain periods of the year which vary according to the particular zone, a ship's hull may be immersed no deeper than her winter load line.

seaworthiness   fitness of a ship for a particular voyage with a particular cargo. The main requirements for seaworthiness are that a ship has sufficient crew, stores and fuel, that machinery and equipment are in good repair and that the ship is fit to receive and carry the cargo.

seaworthy   said of a ship, to be fit for a particular voyage with a particular cargo. *See also* **seaworthiness** *above.*

seconds   measure of the viscosity of oils such as fuel or diesel according to the Redwood Scale. The higher the number of seconds, the greater the viscosity of the oil.

secs.   *see* **seconds.**

119

secure (to)   to prevent a cargo from shifting in transit, usually by lashing it to the ship or to the container or vehicle by means of wires, chains, ropes or straps.

segregated ballast tank   tank in a tanker which is used for water ballast only. There is thus no risk of cargo being mixed with ballast with resulting pollution when the latter is pumped out.

self-propelled barge   barge which has its own motor.

self-sustaining ship   containership which has her own crane for loading and discharging shipping containers enabling the ship to serve ports which do not have suitable lifting equipment.

self-trimming ship   ship whose holds are shaped in such a way that the cargo levels itself.

self-unloader   bulk carrier which is equipped with gear for unloading cargo.

separation   means of identifying separate consignments, particularly where there are several of the same commodity, so that they are not mixed or discharged at the wrong port. This is achieved by, for example, painting different colour marks on the cargo or putting tarpaulins between consignments.

service agreement *or* **service contract**   agreement between a shipper and a liner conference in which the shipper undertakes to ship some or all, as the case may be, of his cargo on conference line ships for a specific period of time in return for an agreed rate of freight and level of service. Some contracts require the shipper to achieve a minimum quantity of cargo over the agreed period.

s.g.   *see* **specific gravity**.

shears *or* **shear-legs**   lifting apparatus, having two uprights separated at the bottom but joined at the top, used for heavy weights. Sometimes spelled **sheers** and **sheer-legs**.

sheers *or* **sheer-legs**   *see* **shears** *above*.

shelter-deck   deck situated above the main deck of a ship.

shelter-deck ship *or* **shelter decker**   ship which has a deck, called the shelter-deck, above her main deck. The original purpose was to enable the ship to benefit from a lower registered tonnage since the shelter-deck space would not be included provided that there was a small opening, known as the tonnage opening, in the upper deck. More recently, such ships have been assigned alternative tonnages and have a tonnage mark painted on their sides. If this mark is submerged, the ship's higher registered tonnage is used for the purpose of determining port charges; if not submerged, the lower tonnage applies.

s.h.e.x.   *see* **Sundays and holidays excepted**.

shift   regular period of work during the course of a day, such as 0600 hours to 1400 hours by, for example, the dockers in a port.

shift (to)   (1)   said of a ship, to move from one place to another, for example, from one berth to another within the same port or from anchorage to berth. In a voyage charter, provision should be made as to whether the time taken to shift counts as laytime.

shift (to)   (2)   said of cargo, to move within the hold of a ship while at sea as a result of insufficient securing or heavy weather. If, in the opinion of the master, this movement renders the ship unsafe, he would sail to the nearest port of refuge for the purpose of restowing and/or resecuring.

shifting boards   longitudinal wooden division erected in the hold of a ship to prevent the sideways shifting of a grain cargo.

shifting charges   charges for moving a ship from one place to another within a port, for example, from one berth to another.

s.h.i.n.c.   *see* **Sundays and holidays included**.

ship   (1)   generic term meaning a floating vessel which is self-propelled and capable of carrying cargo or passengers.

ship   (2)   ship interests, such as the owner or disponent owner or the master and crew of the ship. This term is used when distinguishing between cargo and ship, for example, concerning costings or contractual responsibilities.

ship (to)   to put (goods) on board a ship.

ship breaker   person or company whose business is breaking ships up for scrap. Ships purchased for this purpose are normally paid for on the basis of their light displacement tonnage.

ship broker   *see* **shipbroker** *below*.

ship canal artificial waterway constructed either to provide shipping with shorter distances between ports or to enable ocean-going ships to penetrate inland to industrial areas.

ship chandler merchant who supplies ships with stores and provisions.

ship management business of manning, equipping, provisioning and maintaining a ship. This function may be performed by the shipowner's own organization or by a firm of ship managers.

ship routing service offered by a government department or private company whereby a shipowner or ship operator is provided with a route for his ship, devised by means of up-to-date weather predictions, which avoids severe weather conditions such as storms, fog and ice. This route is normally not the most direct but is expected to take less time since it avoids conditions which would require a reduction in speed. Additionally, the risks of heavy weather damage and, in extreme cases, of injury to the crew, are reduced. A fee is charged for this service. Also known as **weather routing**.

shipbroker person having one of several occupations: **chartering agent** or **owner's broker**, negotiating the terms for the charter of a ship on behalf of a charterer or shipowner respectively; **sale and purchase broker**, negotiating on behalf of a buyer or seller of a ship; **ship's agent**, attending to the requirements of a ship, her master and crew while in port on behalf of the shipowner; **loading broker**, whose business is to attract cargoes to the ships of his principal. Sometimes spelled **ship broker**.

shipbroking the work of a shipbroker. *See* **shipbroker** *above*.

shipchandler merchant who supplies ships with stores and provisions.

shiploader machine used to load a bulk cargo into a ship. It normally consists of a conveyor and chute and is capable of high speed loading.

shipmaster commander of a merchant ship.

shipment putting of goods on board a ship.

shipped (on board) bill of lading bill of lading issued when the goods have been loaded on board the ship. This type of bill of lading, which must contain a reference to the goods having been shipped or shipped on board, is often required by banks who advance money using the bill of lading as collateral security and who wish to be satisfied that the goods are on board the ship.

shipper   person or company who enters into a contract with a liner conference, shipping line or shipowner for the carriage of goods.

shippers' council   body which represents the views and interests of shippers in discussions and negotiations with liner conferences, ports, shipowners' organizations, governments and other bodies involved in the carriage of goods by sea and air.

shipping   (1) maritime transport.

shipping   (2) ships.

shipping   (3) the loading on board a ship (of goods).

shipping conference   *see* **conference**.

shipping instructions   document, prepared by the shipper, which provides the freight forwarder with full instructions regarding the consignment. It includes a description of the cargo, its place of origin and final destination, documentary requirements, the name of the carrying ship, the place and date of loading and any special provisions.

shipping line   company which operates a ship or ships between advertised ports on a regular basis and offers space for goods in return for freight based on a tariff of rates.

shipping mark   markings distinctly displayed on goods being shipped, or on their packaging, for ease of identification. These include the port or place of destination and a package number, if there is more than one.

shipping note   document, completed by the shipper and sent to the shipping line or its agent, detailing the consignment being sent forward for shipment.

ship's agency   business of looking after the interests of a ship while she is in port. *See also* **ship's agent** *below*.

ship's agent   person who looks after the interests of a ship while she is in port. His duties include the arranging of pilotage, towage and a berth for the ship, the signing of bills of lading and the collection of freight. The agent is paid a fee, agreed in advance with the shipowner.

ship's articles   written agreement between the master of a ship and the crew concerning their employment. It includes rates of pay and capacity of each crewman, the date of commencement of the voyage and its duration. This agreement is also known as the **articles of agreement**.

ship's dues   charge, based on a ship's register tonnage, which contributes towards the capital and operating costs of a port.

ship's gear   crane(s) or derrick(s) fixed to the deck of a ship for loading and discharging cargo and/or stores and spares. It is used for cargo at ports where there are no shore cranes or where the shore cranes are inefficient or of inadequate lifting capacity.

ship's husband   person employed by a shipowner to attend to the maintenance and repair of a ship.

ship's rail   side of a ship. Under many contracts of sale, concluded on f.o.b., c. & f. and c.i.f. terms, including those which incorporate Incoterms, risk passes from seller to buyer when the goods cross the ship's rail at the port of loading.

ship's sweat   condensation which occurs when a ship sails from a warm to a relatively cool climate. The temperature of the cargo drops at a slower rate than that of the ship's environment. Moisture condenses on the inner surfaces of the ship and drips on to the cargo. To avoid damage to cargo caused by ship's sweat, it is important for cargo to be dry when loaded into the ship and ventilation is favoured when meeting these climatic conditions.

ship's tackle   ship's equipment, such as ropes and pulleys, used for lifting.

shipyard   place where ships are built.

shore gear   cranes, situated on the quay, used for loading cargo to, or discharging cargo from, ships. Before a shipowner or charterer schedules or nominates a ship for a particular port, it is necessary to determine whether the port is equipped with cranes and that these are of sufficient capacity to lift the cargo, failing which a ship which has lifting gear is required.

short form bill of lading   bill of lading which does not have printed on it the full terms and conditions of the contract of carriage but instead contains a reference to the carrier's conditions, normally stating that a copy is available on request.

short sea   short distance international trade. Goods in this trade are carried by relatively small ships known as **short sea traders**.

short ship (to)   *see* **shut out (to)** *below*.

short shipment   part of a consignment which has not been shipped in a specific ship, normally because there was insufficient space in the ship or because the goods arrived at the port of loading after the ship had completed loading or had sailed.

short ton   ton of 2,000 lbs. Also referred to as a **net ton**.

shortage   goods shown on the ship's manifest which cannot be found when the ship discharges her cargo.

shortlanded cargo   cargo, shown on the ship's manifest, which has not been discharged at the port for which it was intended. The ship's agent at the discharge port sends a cargo tracer, by letter or telex, to the agents at the other discharge ports on the ship's itinerary to determine whether this cargo was landed in error at one of these ports.

shut out (to)   to fail to take cargo on a ship. Situations where cargo is left behind at the loading port occur mainly when a shipping line has insufficient space on board its ship for the volume of bookings taken, or when cargo arrives after the ship has completed loading. Also referred to as **to short ship**.

side door   watertight barrier which seals an opening in the side of a roll-on roll-off ship through which rolling cargo is wheeled or driven along a ramp into or out of the ship.

side door container   shipping container whose doors are at the side rather than at one end. These containers are used when cargo is required to be loaded or discharged at places where access to the end of the container is difficult.

side ramp   inclined plane which connects the side of a roll-on roll-off ship to the shore or quay on which rolling cargo is wheeled or driven into or off the ship.

sim. sub.   *see* **similar substitute**.

similar substitute   ship offered by a shipowner to a charterer as a replacement for the one originally chartered which is similar in respect of deadweight, capacities and hold and hatch sizes.

simplification (of a tariff)   reduction in the number of classes or categories in the tariff of a shipping line or liner conference to make freighting simpler to administer.

single deck ship *or* **single decker**   ship with one deck, that is, with no horizontal divisions within the hold(s). An example of a single deck ship is a bulk carrier.

sister ship   ship with the same specification as another. This is sometimes offered to a charterer by a shipowner who has two or more identical ships but is not certain at the time of negotiating the charter which ship will be in the most suitable geographical position to perform the voyage.

skids   pieces of wood attached to the underside of a heavy package to facilitate mechanical handling.

slack water   still or almost still water when the tide is neither coming in nor going out.

slewing crane   crane whose jib can be swung to one side or the other.

slewing ramp   ramp of a roll-on roll-off ship which is capable of being swung to either side to enable cargo to be rolled on and off from a variety of berthing positions at different ports.

sling   rope or chain placed around goods and attached to the hook of a crane for the purpose of loading and discharging. Some rope slings incorporate a piece of canvas or wood to support the goods.

sling (to)   to surround goods with a sling for the purpose of loading or discharging.

slop tank   tank in a tanker into which slops are pumped. These represent a residue of the ship's cargo of oil together with the water used to clean the cargo tanks. They are left to separate out in the slop tank.

slops   residue of a ship's cargo of oil together with the water used to clean the cargo tanks.

slot   compartment in the hold of a containership into which a shipping container fits exactly. Also referred to as a **cell**.

slot charter   the chartering in of a ship by a fleet operator for a specific voyage when none of the ships in the fleet is available.

slot charter (to)   as a fleet operator, to charter in a ship for a specific voyage when none of the ships in the fleet is available.

126

slow steam (to)   to reduce the speed of a ship in order to make savings in fuel costs. These savings are offset to some degree by the extra running costs incurred as a result of the lengthening of the voyage.

snotter   length of rope with an eye at each end used for lifting bagged cargoes.

socket   point of a ship's electrical power supply to which a refrigerated container is connected.

sole arbitrator   individual who, in accordance with a contract such as a charter-party, is alone nominated by both parties to settle a dispute arising out of the contract. *See also* **arbitrator**.

sous palan   under ship's tackle. This term qualifies a freight rate and may apply to the port of loading or discharging. At the loading port, it signifies that the shipowner's responsibility commences when the goods are delivered alongside, under the ship's tackle. At the discharging port, it signifies that the shipowner's responsibility ends when the goods are lifted off the ship and on to the quay.

Sovcoal   voyage charter-party, published by the Baltic and International Maritime Conference (B.I.M.C.O.), used for shipments of coal from the U.S.S.R.

Sovcoalbill   bill of lading intended to be used for shipments of coal from the U.S.S.R. under the Sovcoal charter-party.

Sovconround   voyage charter-party, published by the Chamber of Shipping of the United Kingdom, used for shipments of timber from the U.S.S.R.

Sovconroundbill   bill of lading intended to be used for shipments of timber from the U.S.S.R. under the Sovconround charter-party.

Sovietwood   voyage charter-party, published by the Baltic and International Maritime Conference (B.I.M.C.O.), used for shipments of wood from the U.S.S.R.

Sovorecon   voyage charter-party, published by the Shipchartering Coordinating Bureau, Moscow, used for shipments of ores and concentrates from the U.S.S.R.

Sovoreconbill   bill of lading intended to be used for shipments of ores and ore concentrates from the U.S.S.R. under the Sovorecon charter-party.

127

s.p.   *see* **safe port**.

s. & p.   sale and purchase.

spar ceiling   strips of timber fixed to the frames of a ship, often horizontally but sometimes vertically, to keep cargo away from the sides of the ship, to avoid both damage and condensation. Also known as **cargo battens** and **permanent dunnage**.

s.p.d.   steamer pays dues.

special commodity quotation   reduction in the tariff freight rate offered by a liner conference to a shipper, normally for one particular commodity, when the application of the full tariff rate would make it difficult for the shipper to achieve or maintain a certain level of shipments because of its effect on the competitiveness of the selling price.

special survey   stringent examination of a ship's hull and machinery carried out every five years by a classification society surveyor for the purpose of maintaining class.

specific gravity   ratio of the weight of a liquid to its cubic capacity.

spot   said of a ship which is available to load almost immediately.

spout   pipe which projects beyond the quay and over the hatchway of a ship and directs bulk cargoes such as grain into the hold.

spout trimmed   said of a bulk cargo, levelled in the hold(s) of a ship simply by moving the spout, which is used to load the cargo, to and fro. *See also* **spout** *above*.

spreader   device, normally constructed of steel, to which chains are secured, all of which is attached to the cargo to be loaded or discharged. By virtue of the shape of the spreader, the chains are spread which makes the lifting and handling of the cargo safer and more efficient. Spreaders are used with awkwardly shaped or long length cargoes. They are also used with shipping containers when loading or discharging is required to be carried out with a jib crane.

spring tide   tide whose range between high and low water is at its highest.

square of the hatch   area of the hold of a ship directly below the hatchway.

Goods are stowed in this area if they require to be lifted from the ship without first having to be moved into position under the crane.

squat (to) said of a ship, to increase draught when reducing speed.

s.s.h.e.x. *see* **Saturdays, Sundays and holidays excepted**.

s.s.h.i.n.c. *see* **Saturdays, Sundays and holidays included**.

stackable flat flatrack which, when empty, may be interlocked with other similar empty flatracks into a stack which has the same dimensions as a single standard shipping container, enabling them to be transported in the same way. Flats which are stackable in this way are known as **collapsible flatracks** when they have corner posts which are collapsed when not in use, and **folding flatracks** when they have ends which are folded down. Both types are designed for the carriage of cargoes of awkward size.

stanchion pillar in the hold of a ship supporting a deck.

starboard right side of a ship when facing the front or forward end.

statement of facts statement, prepared by the ship's agent at the loading and discharging ports, which shows the dates and times of arrival of the ship and the commencement and completion of loading and discharging. It details the quantity of cargo loaded or discharged each day, the hours worked and the hours stopped with the reasons for the stoppages, such as bad weather, a strike or breakdown of equipment. Sometimes referred to as a **port log**.

s.t.c. *see* **said to contain**.

stem (1) the foremost part of a ship.

stem (2) availability of a cargo on the date or dates on which a ship is offering to load.

stem a berth (to) to reserve a berth for a ship.

stem bunkers (to) to contract for the supply of bunkers.

stern the aftermost part of a ship.

stern ramp inclined plane which connects the after end of a roll-on roll-off ship with the shore or quay on which rolling cargo is wheeled or driven on to or off the ship. The ramp is very often designed to make a watertight door to cover the opening in the ship.

stern door   watertight barrier which seals an opening in the after end of a roll-on roll-off ship through which rolling cargo is wheeled or driven along a ramp into or off the ship. This door is often made up of the ramp itself which is operated hydraulically.

stevedore   person running a business whose functions are to load, stow and unload ships.

stevedoring charges   charges for loading and stowing or unloading a ship, as the case may be.

stiff   said of a ship, having a tendency to roll quickly due to a large metacentric height often caused by stowing dense cargoes low in a ship.

stoppage in transitu   right of an unpaid seller of goods to order a master to deliver those goods back to him should the buyer become insolvent while the goods are in transit.

stow   position in a ship where goods are placed for their carriage to the port of discharge. *See also* **stowage** *below*.

stow (to)   to arrange or position goods in a ship for their carriage to the port of discharge. *See also* **stowage** *below*.

stow deadweight (to)   said of a cargo, to take up less than one cubic metre of space in a ship for each tonne of cargo.

stowage   the placing of goods in a ship in such a way as to ensure, firstly, the safety and stability of the ship not only on a sea or ocean passage but also in between ports when parts of the cargo have been loaded or discharged, as the case may be; secondly, the safety of the individual consignments which should not be damaged or contaminated by being in proximity to goods with which they are not compatible; thirdly, the ability to unload goods at their port of discharge without having to move goods destined for other ports.

stowage factor   ratio of a cargo's cubic measurement to its weight, expressed in cubic feet to the ton or cubic metres to the tonne. The stowage factor is used in conjunction with a ship's grain or bale capacities to determine the total quantity of cargo which can be loaded.

stowage plan   plan, in the form of a longitudinal cross-section of a ship, which shows the locations in the ship of all the consignments. It is frequently colour-coded to highlight the various ports of discharge. The stowage plan is very often sent to the stevedore at each of the discharge ports to assist them in planning the discharging of the ship.

straddle carrier   wheeled vehicle designed to lift and carry shipping containers within its own framework. It is used for moving, and sometimes stacking, shipping containers at a container terminal.

strand (to)   said of a ship, to cease moving as a result of touching the bottom.

stranding   contact by a ship with the bottom which prevents her from moving. Stranding is normally an involuntary act but it also occurs when a ship is intentionally run ashore to avoid a greater peril.

strengthened hold   hold of a ship whose tank top is reinforced to carry dense cargoes such as ores.

strike clause   clause in a bill of lading or charter-party which sets out the options available to the parties to the contract of carriage in the event that a strike prevents or interrupts the loading or discharging of the cargo. The wording of the clause and the options vary according to the individual contract. In the case of a charter, the clause may contain a provision for the effect of a strike on laytime.

strike-bound   (1) said of a port where no loading or discharging is taking place because of a strike of dockers or where ships are unable to enter or leave because of a strike of pilots, tugmen or lock-gatemen.

strike-bound   (2) said of a ship which is unable to leave a port because of a strike of pilots, tugmen or lock-gatemen.

string of barges   group of barges tied together for towing.

strip a container (to)   to unload a shipping container.

stripping pump   pump in a tanker used towards completion of discharge to pump out the remaining cargo.

stuff (to)   to load a shipping container.

sub.   (1) subject. *For examples, see under* **subject**.

131

sub. (2) substitute. *For definition, see* **substitute** *and* **substitution** *below.*

sub-charter *see* **sub-let.**

sub-charter (to) *see* **sub-let (to).**

sub-charterer person or company who charters a ship from a party who is not the owner but who, in turn, has chartered the ship.

sub-freight freight payable by the sub-charterer, normally to the charterer. *See also* **sub-charterer** *and* **sub-let.**

subject details *or* **sub. details** term qualifying an offer or counter-offer for the charter of a ship which denotes that only minor details remain to be agreed. It is widely accepted that the conclusion of a contract is conditional on these details being agreed although an American court has ruled that the acceptance of such an offer or counter-offer is sufficient to create a contract, leaving the details to be agreed subsequently.

subject free *or* **sub. free** term used in an offer made by a shipowner to signify that the acceptance of that offer will only result in a contract if one has not been concluded in the meantime with a third party. Also referred to as **subject open** or **subject unfixed.**

subject open *or* **sub. open** *see* **subject free** *above.*

subject stem *or* **sub. stem** subject to the availability of the cargo on the date or dates on which a ship is offering to load.

subject unfixed *or* **sub. unfixed** *see* **subject free** *above.*

sub-let the charter of a ship to one party by another party who is not the owner but who, in turn, has chartered the ship. Also referred to as a **sub-charter.**

sub-let (to) said of a charterer of a ship, to charter or hire the ship out to another party. Also referred to as **to recharter** and **to sub-charter.**

subrogation transfer to the insurer of the rights of an insured to recover from an ocean carrier or other responsible party for loss or damage to cargo.

substitute replacement ship for a particular voyage. *See also* **substitution** *below.*

132

substitute (to) to replace a ship, chartered for a particular voyage, with another. *See also* **substitution** *below*.

substitution the replacement of a ship with another ship. A shipowner often has an option in a voyage charter to employ a ship other than the one named in the charter-party since he may not know which of his ships will be capable of performing the voyage at the time the contract is concluded, particularly if this is done well in advance of loading.

suction elevator method of unloading bulk cargoes of grain from ships by pneumatic suction.

suit time period within which cargo interests must bring a lawsuit against the carrier for any claim which they have under the contract of carriage. Failing this, the carrier is normally discharged of all liability. The period may vary according to the particular contract but is often one year from the date when the goods were delivered or should have been delivered. In practice, many claims are not fully quantified in time and the carrier can grant an extension to suit time on the request of cargo interests to provide the parties with further time to settle the claim out of court.

summer freeboard distance between the deck line and the appropriate load line for a ship in a summer zone. *See also* **freeboard** *and* **load line zone**.

summer load line line painted on the sides of a ship which shows the maximum depth to which that ship's hull may be immersed when in a summer zone. The line is marked with an S. Also referred to as the **Plimsoll line** or **summer marks**. *See also* **load line zone**.

summer marks *see* **summer load line** *above*.

summer tanks upper wing tanks of a tanker.

summer timber freeboard distance between the deck line and the appropriate load line for a ship with a deck cargo of timber in a summer zone. *See also* **freeboard** *and* **load line zone**.

summer timber load line line painted on the sides of a ship which shows the maximum depth to which that ship's hull may be immersed when in a summer zone with a deck cargo of timber. This line is marked LS. *See also* **load line zone**.

summer zone one of several geographical areas defined by the International

Conference on Load Lines, where a ship's hull may be immersed no deeper than her summer load line.

Sundays and holidays excepted charter-party term which provides that Sundays and public holidays do not count in the calculation of laytime. *See also* **even if used** *and* **unless used**.

Sundays and holidays included charter-party term which provides that Sundays and public holidays count in the calculation of laytime, whether or not used for loading or discharging, as the case may be.

supercargo person employed by a shipowner or shipping company or charterer of a ship or shipper of goods to supervise cargo handling operations.

supervisory agent person or company appointed by a shipowner to protect his interests and to supervise the work carried out by the ship's agent when the owner's ship is in port. The ship's agent may be the only agent at the port or he may have been appointed or nominated by the charterer and therefore not the choice of the shipowner. Also referred to as a **protecting agent** or **protective agent**.

supplementary call extra payment, made by a shipowner to the protection and indemnity association with which his ship is entered, to cover claims made by all the shipowning members against the association's funds which were not allowed for in the yearly advance call. The amount is generally based on the ship's tonnage.

Supplytime time charter-party, published by the Baltic and International Maritime Conference (B.I.M.C.O.), used for offshore service ships.

s.w.a.d. salt water arrival draught.

sweat condensation which occurs either when a ship sails from a cool to a relatively warm climate (*see* **cargo sweat**) or vice versa (*see* **ship's sweat**). Often, the expert use of ventilation is required to prevent sweat which can cause serious damage to cargoes.

sweep the holds (to) to clear rubbish from the holds of a ship after a cargo has been discharged so that they are clean in readiness for the next cargo. It is often a requirement of time charter-parties that the holds of the ship be clean or clean-swept on delivery to the time charterer at the beginning of the period of the charter and, similarly, on redelivery to the shipowner at the end of the charter.

s.w.l.   *see* **safe working load.**

sworn shipbroker   official in certain ports in France who has a monopoly, in the port in which he carries on business, in chartering negotiations. Other monopolies enjoyed include the translation of official and other documents, such as charter-parties and bills of lading, sale and purchase of ships and the formalities associated with the inward and outward clearance of ships.

Synacomex   voyage charter-party, whose full name is the Continent Grain Charter Party, used for shipments of grain.

T

t.   (1) tonnes, that is, metric tons of 1,000 kilogrammes.

t.   (2) tropical.

T.A. round   trans-Atlantic round voyage.

taking inward pilot   frequently used provision in a time charter to determine the time and place of delivery of a ship by the owner to the charterer. The hire charge commences at the moment the pilot embarks.

tally   physical count of the number of pieces of cargo loaded into, or discharged from, a ship. *See also* **tally (to)** *below*.

tally (to)   to record the number of pieces together with their description, marks and numbers at the time they are loaded into, or discharged from, a ship. This task may be performed by tally clerks working for the shipowner, the shipper or receiver, or the stevedores. The entries are made on **tally sheets** or in **tally books** and serve to verify the quantity of cargo loaded and discharged.

tally clerk   person employed by a shipping company, shipper, receiver or stevedore to carry out a physical count of cargo being loaded into, or discharged from, a ship. *See also* **tally (to)** *above*.

tally sheet *or* **tally book**   written record of the count of the number of pieces of cargo, their description, marks and numbers, carried out at the time they are loaded into, or discharged from, a ship. *See also* **tally (to)** *above*.

tandem   two cranes are said to be worked **in tandem** when they are employed together so as to make use of their combined lifting capacity when handling lifts in excess of their individual capacities.

tank barge   river barge designed for the carriage of liquid bulk cargoes.

tank car   container used for carrying liquids in bulk by rail.

tank cleaning   removal of all traces of a cargo from the tanks of a tanker normally by means of high pressure water jets.

tank container   shipping container designed for the carriage of liquids. It consists of a cylindrical tank surrounded by a framework which provides the same overall dimensions as those of a standard dry cargo container enabling it to be transported and handled in the same way. Tank containers are insulated, can carry hazardous and non-hazardous liquids and may have facilities for steam heating.

tank top   floor of the hold, so called as it is the top of the double bottom tank.

tanker   ship designed for the carriage of liquid in bulk, her cargo space consisting of several, or indeed many, tanks. Tankers carry a variety of products including crude oil, refined products, liquid gas and wine. Size and capacity range from the ultra large crude carrier (u.l.c.c.) of over half a million tonnes deadweight to the small coastal tanker. Tankers load their cargo by gravity from the shore or by shore pumps and discharge using their own pumps.

tanker broker   shipbroker who specializes in the negotiations for the charter of tankers.

tanker charter   charter-party covering the hire of a tanker. There are various types, for both voyage and time charters, many of which are produced and used by the major oil companies.

tare (weight)   weight of packing or of a shipping container. This is deducted from the gross weight in order to obtain the net weight of the goods.

tariff   schedule of charges, such as the freight tariff of a shipping line or liner conference, in which are published freight rates, generally for a wide variety of commodities.

tariff currency   currency of a particular country on which the freight rates in the tariff of a shipping line or liner conference are based and in which the rates are quoted. Generally, the freight payable by a shipper is converted by the shipping line to the currency of the country of shipment at the rate of exchange ruling on the date of shipment. The most widely used tariff currency world-wide is the U.S. Dollar.

t.b.n.   to be nominated. *See under* **nominate a ship (to)**.

t.d.w.   *see* **total deadweight**.

telegraphic transfer   transfer of funds from a bank in one country to a bank in another country, effected by telegraph or cable.

tender   said of a ship, unstable due to having a small metacentric height with a tendency to roll slowly, often caused by stowing dense cargoes too high.

tender notice of readiness (to)   as master of a ship, to present cargo interests or their agent with written notice that the ship has arrived and is ready to load or discharge, as the case may be. Some charter-parties provide that this notice may be offered at certain times only, for example, during office hours.

terminal handling charge   charge payable to a shipping line either for receiving a full container load at the container terminal, storing it and delivering it to the ship at the load port or for receiving it from the ship at the discharge port, storing it and delivering it to the consignee.

t.e.u.   *see* **twenty foot equivalent unit**.

t.f.   tropical fresh.

through bill of lading   bill of lading issued by a shipping line for a voyage requiring on-carriage, thus involving at least one transhipment. According to the particular contract, the issuer of the bill of lading may be responsible for the goods throughout the voyage or only for one leg, acting as agent for the on-carriage.

through rate   freight rate which includes the ocean carriage, transhipment, if any, and on-carriage by a different means of transport to an inland destination.

tidal range   difference in the depth of water between low water and the next or previous high water.

tide tables   tidal predictions for a port, published by the port authority, giving dates and depths of water, often covering a period of one calendar year.

tier limit *or* **tier limitation**   maximum number of levels of a commodity which may be stowed on top of each other without suffering damage from compression.

timber carrier   ship designed for the carriage of timber, usually geared and having large hatchways. Sometimes referred to as a **forest products carrier.**

timber load line   one of the lines painted on the sides of a ship which show the maximum depths to which that ship's hull may be immersed when arriving at, sailing through or putting to sea in the different load line zones with a deck cargo of timber. The positioning of these lines is determined by the rules agreed at the International Conference on Load Lines which have been ratified by many maritime countries.

time   frequently used term to mean laytime. *For definition, see* **laytime.**

time bar   expiry of the period within which a lawsuit must be brought or arbitration commenced against a carrier for any claim under a contract of carriage. Normally, a claim which is the subject of a time bar will not succeed. This period is agreed in the contract of carriage and can be extended by agreement of the two parties.

time charter   (1) the hiring of a ship from a shipowner for a period of time. Under this type of contract, the shipowner places his ship, with crew and equipment, at the disposal of the charterer, for which the charterer pays hire money. Subject to any restrictions in the contract, the charterer decides the type and quantity of cargo to be carried and the ports of loading and discharging. He is responsible for supplying the ship with bunkers and for the payment of cargo handling operations, port charges, pilotage, towage and ship's agency. The technical operation and navigation of the ship remain the responsibility of the shipowner. A ship hired in this way is said to be **on time charter.**

time charter   (2) abbreviation for time charter-party. *For definition, see* **time charter-party** *below.*

time charter (to)   to hire a ship for a period of time. This may be said either of a shipowner, who hires his ship out to a charterer, or of a charterer who hires a ship from a shipowner. *See also* **time charter** (1) *above.*

time charterer   person or company who hires a ship for a period of time. *See also* **time charter** (1) *above.*

time charter-party   document containing the terms and conditions of a

138

contract between a charterer and a shipowner for the hire of a ship for a period of time.

time sheet   statement, drawn up by the ship's agent at the loading and discharging ports, which details the time worked in loading or discharging the cargo together with the amount of laytime used. This latter figure, when compared with the time allowed in the voyage charter-party, is used by the shipowner and charterer to calculate demurrage or despatch, as the case may be.

time-barred   said of a claim against a carrier for which the period within which a lawsuit must be brought, or arbitration commenced, has expired. Normally, a time-barred claim will not succeed.

time-charter   alternative spelling of time charter. *For definition, see* **time charter** *and* **time charter (to)** *above.*

time-charterer   alternative spelling of time charterer. *For definition, see* **time charterer** *above.*

t.i.r.   transport international routier.

t.l.o.   total loss only.

tolerated outsider   shipping line which, although it is not a member of a particular liner conference, has an agreement with that conference covering the level of service provided, particularly in respect of the freight rates which it offers to shippers who have a loyalty contract with that conference. Shippers are allowed by the conference to ship cargo in ships operated by the tolerated outsider without infringing their loyalty contract.

tomming   shoring of cargo to prevent it from shifting.

ton   2,240 lbs.

tonnage   (1) quantity of cargo, normally expressed as a number of tonnes or tons.

tonnage   (2) cubic capacity of a ship. *See also* **net tonnage** *and* **gross tonnage**.

tonnage   (3) cargo capacity of all the ships of a country or of a particular trade.

tonnage mark   mark on the side of a shelter-deck ship which, depending on whether it is submerged or not, determines whether the ship's larger or smaller register tonnage applies. *See also* **shelter-deck ship**.

tonnage opening   permanent opening in the shelter-deck of a ship designed such that her registered tonnage would not include the shelter-deck space although this space is capable of carrying cargo. *See also* **shelter-deck ship**.

tonne   metric ton of 1,000 kilogrammes.

tonner   ship of a given deadweight. For example, a 2,000 tonner is a ship of 2,000 tonnes deadweight.

tonnes per centimetre   quantity, for example of cargo or fuel, needed to immerse a ship one further centimetre. This quantity varies not only ship by ship but also according to the quantity already on board.

tonnes per day   quantity of cargo loaded or discharged each day. The time allowed by a shipowner to a charterer for loading or discharging, known as laytime, is often expressed as a number of tonnes per day.

tons per inch   quantity, for example of cargo or fuel, needed to immerse a ship one further inch. This quantity varies not only ship by ship but also according to the quantity already on board.

top off (to)   to fill a ship which is already partly loaded with cargo. This operation occurs when there is a draught restriction at the first load port or between there and the open sea. The ship loads a quantity of cargo corresponding to the permissible draught, then fills up at the second port where there is no restriction.

top stow cargo   goods which are stowed on top of all others in a ship's hold because of their relatively low density and the probability that they would be damaged if overstowed.

total deadweight   difference between a ship's loaded and light displacements, consisting of the total weight of cargo, fuel, fresh water, stores and crew which a ship can carry when immersed to a particular load line, normally her summer load line. The deadweight is expressed in tons or tonnes. Also referred to as **deadweight** or **deadweight all told**.

t.p.c.   *see* **tonnes per centimetre**.

t.p.d.   *see* **tonnes per day**.

t.p.i.   *see* **tons per inch**.

tracer   message sent by a ship's agent at one of the discharge ports on a ship's itinerary to the agents at all of the other discharge ports to determine whether cargo, which was shown on the ship's manifest as being for discharge at that port but was not discharged there, had been landed in error at one of the other ports. A similar message may be sent to the agent at the loading port to ascertain whether the cargo was not, in fact, loaded.

tractor   self-propelled vehicle used for towing trailers.

trading limits   geographical limits specified in a time charter-party outside which the charterer is not permitted to order the ship.

trailer   vehicle, on which goods are loaded, towed by a tractor.

tramp (ship)   ship which will call at any port to carry whatever cargoes are available, normally on the basis of a charter or part charter. Such a ship is the opposite of a liner ship which trades on a specific route between advertised ports.

transfer charge   charge made by a shipping line for the loan of its equipment, such as containers or trailers, to a shipper or receiver who provides his own inland haulage. Also referred to as an **equipment handover charge**.

tranship (to)   to transfer goods from one ship to another. *See also* **tranship-ment** *below*.

transhipment   transfer of goods from one ship to another. This transfer may be direct or it may be necessary to discharge the goods on to the quay prior to loading them on to the second ship, or on to vehicles should the second ship be loading at a different berth.

transit cargo   goods which are discharged from a sea-going ship in one country but which are destined for another country.

transit time   time taken for goods to be carried from one place to another.

transship (to) *or* **trans-ship (to)**   alternative spellings for tranship. *For definition, see* **tranship (to)** *above*.

transshipment *or* **trans-shipment**   alternative spellings for transhipment. *For definition, see* **transhipment** *above*.

transverse bulkhead   vertical separation across a ship, for example between two holds.

trim   relationship between a ship's draughts forward and aft. Consideration is given to the trim when loading cargo since it is desirable to sail with a reasonably even keel. Failing this, a ship is safer down by the stern, that is, with the draught aft slightly deeper than the draught forward. Adjustments can be made to the trim by the way in which the cargo is distributed in the hold(s) and by means of water ballast, for example in the peak tanks.

trim cargo (to)   to level a bulk cargo in the hold of a ship in order to contribute to her stability at sea.

trim a ship (to)   to adjust the draughts forward and aft of a ship so as to enable her to sail on a reasonably even keel. This is achieved by careful distribution of cargo in the hold(s) and by means of water ballast, for example in the peak tanks.

trimmed by the head   said of a ship whose draught forward is slightly deeper than her draught aft. This often makes the handling of the ship difficult at sea. Also referred to as **down by the head**.

trimmed by the stern   said of a ship whose draught aft is slightly deeper than her draught forward. Also referred to as **down by the stern**.

trip charter   time charter of a ship for one specific trip, rather than for a period of time. Also used occasionally to mean a voyage charter.

tropical draught   depth of water to which a ship may be immersed in a tropical zone as indicated by the tropical load line painted on the side of the ship in accordance with load line regulations.

tropical freeboard   distance between the deck line and the appropriate load line for a ship in a tropical zone. *See also* **freeboard** *and* **load line zone**.

tropical fresh water load line   line painted on the sides of a ship which shows the maximum depth to which that ship's hull may be immersed when in fresh water in a tropical zone. The line is marked TF. *See also* **load line zone**.

tropical fresh water timber load line   line painted on the sides of a ship which shows the maximum depth to which that ship's hull may be immersed when in fresh water in a tropical zone with a deck cargo of timber. The line is marked LTF. *See also* **load line zone**.

tropical load line   line painted on the sides of a ship which shows the maximum depth to which that ship's hull may be immersed when in a tropical zone. The line is marked T. *See also* **load line zone**.

tropical timber freeboard   distance between the deck line and the appropriate load line for a ship with a deck cargo of timber in a tropical zone. *See also* **freeboard** *and* **load line zone**.

tropical timber load line   line painted on the sides of a ship which shows the maximum depth to which that ship's hull may be immersed when in a tropical zone with a deck cargo of timber. The line is marked LT. *See also* **load line zone**.

tropical zone   one of several geographical areas, defined by the International Conference on Load Lines, where a ship's hull may be immersed no deeper than her tropical load line.

t.t.   *see* **telegraphic transfer**.

tug   small, powerful vessel used for towing or pushing ships in port, towing or pushing barges along rivers or towing, for example, oil rigs out to sea.

turn (a ship) round (to)   to bring a ship into a port, load or discharge her and sail her from the port. This term is most often used in connection with the time taken to carry out this operation.

turn round time *or* **turnround time** *or* **turnaround time**   time between a ship arriving in a port and sailing.

turn time   time during which a ship waits for a berth.

turnbuckle   device which applies tension to ropes or chains used for lashing cargo. Also referred to as a **bottle screw**.

tween deck   deck which separates the hold of a ship into two, making an upper and a lower hold.

tween deck ship *or* **tween decker**   ship with two decks of which the upper one is the main deck.

twenty foot equivalent unit   unit of measurement equivalent to one twenty foot shipping container, normally abbreviated to **t.e.u.** Thus a forty foot container is equal to two t.e.u.'s. This measurement is used to quantify, for

143

example, the container capacity of a ship, the number of containers carried on a particular voyage or over a period of time, or it may be the unit on which freight is payable.

twist lock   device which is inserted into each of the four corner fittings of a shipping container and is turned or twisted, thus locking the container for the purpose of securing or lifting.

U

u.l.c.c.   *see* **ultra large crude carrier.**

ullage   height of the space in a cargo tank above the surface of the liquid cargo. This distance is used to calculate the volume of liquid in the tank.

ullaging   determining the measurement of ullage by means of a measuring tape inserted into the tank.

ultra large crude carrier   giant tanker of no official size but variously described as being one between 350,000 tonnes deadweight and 550,000 tonnes deadweight.

umpire   person who decides a dispute which has been the subject of an arbitration involving two arbitrators who are unable to agree.

unclean bill of lading   bill of lading containing one, or more than one, superimposed clause specifying a defect to the cargo or packing, noted at the time the goods are received by the ship. Such a bill of lading is also referred to as foul or dirty.

uncontainerable *or* **uncontainerizable**   said of cargo which is incapable of being loaded into a shipping container because of its dimensions.

U.N.C.T.A.D.   United Nations Conference on Trade and Development. It is an agency of the United Nations Organization whose work in shipping includes the liner code involving the sharing of cargoes between the shipping lines of the importing and exporting countries and third countries in the ratio 40 : 40 : 20.

under deck shipment   carriage of goods within the hold of a ship, as distinct from their carriage on deck. Under deck shipment affords greater protection against the elements and is often a requirement of purchasers of goods, particularly when payment is by letter of credit.

under-consumption   amount of fuel used per day or over a period of time by a ship which is less than the amount expected or agreed.

underkeel clearance   minimum distance between the bottom of a ship and the bed of a river or sea, required by some authorities as a safety margin because of unseen hazards or climatic changes in the depth of water. Also known as **keel clearance**.

undock (to)   to leave a dock.

union purchase   common method of loading or discharging cargo by combining two derricks, one of which is fixed over the quay, the other over the hatchway. The cargo is lifted by heaving on the appropriate derrick and transferred from ship to shore or vice versa by heaving on the second derrick while slacking on the first one.

unit load   method of presenting goods for shipment such that they are in lifts of regular size or weight, for example goods shipped on pallets or pre-slung. This method simplifies the handling of the cargo and increases the rate of loading and discharging of ships since there will be fewer, and heavier, lifts.

unitization   the grouping of goods for shipment into a unit of regular size, known as a unit load.

unitize (to)   to group goods for shipment into a unit of regular size, known as a unit load, to facilitate handling and increase the rate of loading and discharging of a ship. Goods on pallets, for example, are said to be unitized.

universal bulk carrier   ship designed to carry all types of bulk cargoes. Her size and draught enable her to enter most ports.

unless used   charter-party term which provides that a proportion, normally all or half, of time used to load or discharge, as the case may be, during excepted periods counts for the purpose of calculating total time used.

unload (to)   to remove goods from a ship.

unloader   machine used to unload a bulk cargo from a ship.

145

unmoor (to)   to remove the ropes which attach a ship to the shore.

unprotected   said of goods which are shipped without any protective packing.

unseaworthiness   unfitness of a ship for a particular voyage with a particular cargo. This could be, for example, as a result of insufficiency of crew, stores or fuel, machinery or equipment not being in good repair or unfitness to receive or carry the cargo.

unseaworthy   said of a ship, unfit for a particular voyage with a particular cargo. *See also* **unseaworthiness** *above.*

unstuff (to)   to unload a shipping container.

upper tween deck   space for carrying cargo below the main deck of a ship above the deck which divides the upper hold.

U.S.D.   United States Dollars.

U.S.N.H.   United States North of Hatteras.

utilization   quantity of cargo which can be loaded into a shipping container.

utilization allowance   deduction from the f.c.l. freight provided by a shipping line or liner conference to a shipper who loads a minimum number of tonnes or cubic metres of cargo into a shipping container. There may be various allowances depending on the degree of utilization of the container. Also known as an **f.c.l. allowance**.

u.u.   *see* **unless used.**

V

valorem   *see* **ad valorem freight.**

valuation form   statement, signed by cargo interests, required by a general average adjuster to enable the contributions to general average to be calculated. This form requires details of the voyage to be filled in, together with the cargo and its invoice or shipped value and, if the goods are insured, the name and address of underwriters and the insured value.

valuation scale   list of freight rates, in the tariff of a liner conference or shipping line, each of which is applicable to a range of f.o.b. values; generally, the higher the f.o.b. value per tonne, the higher the freight rate.

v.a.t.   value added tax.

v/c   *see* **voyage charter**.

ventilate (to)   to introduce fresh air into the hold of a ship by means of a ventilator on deck or by opening the hatches or by means of a mechanical system. The purpose of ventilating is to prevent condensation. *See also* **ventilation** *below*.

ventilated container   shipping container designed for the carriage of cargoes which require constant ventilation, such as citrus fruit and coffee. Ventilation is normally achieved by means of small openings in the container.

ventilation   the introduction of fresh air into the hold of a ship. The purpose is to warm or cool the cargo so as to prevent large differences occurring between the temperature of the cargo and that of the ship's environment which would give rise to condensation. Ventilation is effected by means of ventilators of various types attached to the deck of the ship, or in fine weather by opening the hatches, or by a mechanical system which forces air into the hold. Ventilation is also used in certain types of shipping container.

ventilator   duct attached to the deck of a ship which allows fresh air to enter the hold (*see* **ventilation**). Ventilators are of various types, the most common of which is the cowl type which can be swivelled to vary the rate of air flow into as well as out of the hold.

very large crude carrier   large tanker of no official size but variously described as being one between 100,000 tonnes deadweight and 350,000 tonnes deadweight.

vessel   (1) ship or boat.

vessel   (2) vessel interests, such as the owner or disponent owner or the master and crew of the vessel. This term is used when distinguishing between cargo and vessel, for example, concerning costings or contractual responsibilities.

Visconbill   liner bill of lading published by the Baltic and International Maritime Conference (B.I.M.C.O.). *See* **liner bill of lading**.

Visconbooking   liner booking note published by the Baltic and International Maritime Conference (B.I.M.C.O.). *See* **booking note**.

v.l.c.c.   *see* **very large crude carrier**.

voucher   document, such as a receipt, which supports an item on the disbursements account rendered to the shipowner by the ship's agent at a port.

voy.   voyage.

voyage account   statement of the costs and revenue of a voyage of a ship made after the voyage is completed when the income and all actual costs are known.

voyage charter   (1) contract of carriage in which the charterer pays for the use of a ship's cargo space for one, or sometimes more than one, voyage. Under this type of charter, the shipowner pays all the operating costs of the ship while payment for port and cargo handling charges are the subject of agreement between the parties. Freight is generally paid per unit of cargo, such as a tonne, based on an agreed quantity, or as a lump sum irrespective of the quantity loaded. The terms and conditions of the contract are set down in a document known as a charter-party. A ship chartered in this way is said to be **on voyage charter**.

voyage charter   (2) abbreviation for voyage charter-party. *For definition, see* **voyage charter-party** *below*.

voyage charter (to)   to contract for the use of a ship's cargo space for one, or more than one, voyage. This may be said of a shipowner or of a charterer. *See also* **voyage charter** (1) *above*.

voyage charter-party   document containing the terms and conditions of a contract between a charterer and a shipowner for the use of a ship's cargo space for one, or more than one, voyage.

voyage estimate   calculation of the profitability of a prospective voyage of a ship using estimated figures. In the case of a tramp shipowner, the estimate is used to compare two or more possible voyages in order to determine which is the most profitable. Similarly, a time charterer would compare two or more ships so as to charter the one which is least costly overall. The content of an estimate varies according to the type and terms of the charter and whether the calculation is being made by a shipowner or charterer. The principal costs are the running cost of the ship (or hire money for a time charterer), bunker costs, port charges and canal dues together with ship's agency fees and any cargo handling costs. The revenue is the daily hire, in the case of a time charter, or the freight, less any commission.

W

w. (1) weight.

w. (2) winter.

wagon demurrage charge made by the railways on the user of a railway wagon for detaining it beyond the agreed time.

war clause clause in a bill of lading or charter-party which sets out the course of action open to the master of a ship in the event that the ship or her cargo or crew would be put at risk because of war should the voyage proceed. The clause varies according to individual contracts but invariably the master would not be required to put his ship or crew at risk.

warp (to) to shift a ship by means of her mooring ropes.

water ballast heavy weight of sea water carried by a ship when without a cargo for stability and safety at sea.

water density ratio of the weight of water to its volume. This ranges from 1,000 kilogrammes per cubic metre for fresh water to 1,026 kilogrammes for sea water, with brackish water in between. Sea water provides greater buoyancy than fresh water so a ship loaded in fresh water to her fresh water load line will rise to her summer load line by the time she reaches the open sea.

waybill document, issued by a shipping line to a shipper, which serves as a receipt for the goods and evidence of the contract of carriage. In these respects it resembles a bill of lading but, unlike a bill of lading, it is not a document of title; it bears the name of the consignee who has only to identify himself in order to take delivery of the cargo. Because it is not negotiable, the waybill is not acceptable to banks as collateral security. The purpose of the waybill is to avoid the delays to ships' and cargoes which occur when bills of lading are late in arriving at the discharge port. This document is also referred to as a **liner waybill** or an **ocean waybill** or a **sea waybill**.

weather deck   uppermost deck, extending the length of a ship, which is exposed to the weather.

weather permitting   term used in a voyage charter to signify that laytime does not count when weather conditions do not allow loading or discharging operations to be carried out.

weather routing   service offered by a government department or private company whereby a shipowner or ship operator is provided with a route for his ship, devised by means of up-to-date weather predictions, which avoids severe weather conditions such as storms, fog and ice. This route is normally not the most direct but is expected to take less time since it avoids conditions which would require a reduction in speed. Additionally, the risks of heavy weather damage and, in extreme cases, of injury to the crew, are reduced. A fee is charged for this service. Also known as **ship routing**.

weather working day   day on which work is normally carried out at a port and which counts as laytime unless loading or discharging would have ceased because of bad weather.

weather-bound   said of a ship which is unable to sail from a port or place because the severity of the weather would make sailing unsafe.

w.e.f.   with effect from. This is said, for example, of the date when a new or amended surcharge of a shipping line takes effect.

weight cargo   cargo one tonne of which measures one cubic metre or less. Freight on a weight cargo is generally payable on the weight, that is, per tonne or per ton. Also referred to as **deadweight cargo**.

weight or measure(ment)   freight for a consignment payable on the basis of its weight or cubic measurement, whichever provides the carrier with the greater return.

weight rated cargo   cargo whose freight is payable on the basis of its weight, by means of a rate per tonne. Weight rated cargoes are generally, although not always, those which measure less than one cubic metre to one tonne. The freight for such cargoes is said to be payable **on the weight**.

weight/measurement ratio   ratio of a cargo's weight to its cubic measurement, expressed in cubic feet to the ton or cubic metres to the tonne. This ratio can be used in conjunction with a ship's bale or grain capacities to determine the total quantity of cargo which can be loaded in a ship.

Welcon   voyage charter-party, published by the Chamber of Shipping of the United Kingdom, used for shipments of coal.

well   (1) depression in a specially designed flatrack into which steel coils rest to prevent them from moving when in transit.

well   (2) space between the forecastle and the bridge or between the poop and the bridge.

wet weight   weight of a bulk cargo including its moisture content.

wharf   structure built alongside the water where ships berth for loading or discharging goods.

wharfage (charges)   charges payable by cargo interests for the use of a wharf.

wharfinger   person who owns or operates a wharf.

when where ready   frequently used provision in a time charter to determine the time and place of redelivery of a ship by the charterer to the shipowner. This term is qualified in such a way as to make the time and place unambiguous, such as on completion of discharge at a named port.

whether in berth or not   provision in a voyage charter that, once the ship has arrived at the port and tendered notice of readiness, if required, laytime will start to count in accordance with the charter-party whether or not the ship has reached the berth.

whether in free pratique or not   provision in a voyage charter that, once the ship has arrived at the port and tendered notice of readiness, if required, laytime will start to count in accordance with the charter-party whether or not pratique has been granted by the authorities.

whether in port or not   provision in a voyage charter that the ship does not need to be within the port limits for laytime to start to count. She need only arrive at the anchorage, if outside the port, and tender notice of readiness, if required, for laytime to start to count in accordance with the charter-party.

white products   refined products such as aviation spirit, motor spirit and kerosene. Also referred to as **clean (petroleum) products**.

w.i.b.o.n.   *see* **whether in berth or not** *above.*

wide laycan   large spread of dates between the first of the laydays and the last. A shipowner may offer his ship with a wide laycan in order to minimize the risk of the ship arriving after the cancelling date which would normally give the charterer the right to cancel the charter.

w.i.f.p.o.n.   *see* **whether in free pratique or not** *above.*

winch clause   clause in a charter-party which makes a provision for the use of the ship's winches by the charterer. The clause often includes a stipulation as to the number of winchmen to be made available by the shipowner and the responsibility for payment of shore winches, if these are used.

windage   quantity of cargo blown away by the wind during loading or discharging. This type of loss occurs to fine bulk cargoes.

wine tanker   ship designed to carry cargoes of wine in bulk. Such ships are capable of carrying several grades of wine at the same time and usually have stainless steel tanks.

wing   the side of a ship's hold.

wing tank   tank situated at the side of a ship such as a tanker, bulk carrier or combination carrier. Unlike the wing tank of a tanker which extends the entire depth of the cargo space, that of a bulk carrier or combination carrier is most often located at the top of the hold and may be used for bulk cargoes such as grain, or for water ballast.

winter freeboard   distance between the deck line and the appropriate load line for a ship in a winter zone. *See also* **freeboard** *and* **load line zone**.

winter load line   line painted on the sides of a ship which shows the maximum depth to which that ship's hull may be immersed when in a winter zone. Also referred to as **winter marks**. The line is marked W. *See also* **load line zone**.

winter marks   *see* **winter load line** *above.*

winter North Atlantic freeboard   distance between the deck line and the appropriate load line for a ship in winter in one of the North Atlantic winter seasonal zones. *See also* **freeboard** *and* **load line zone**.

winter North Atlantic load line   line painted on the sides of a ship which shows the maximum depth to which that ship's hull may be immersed when in

152

one of the North Atlantic winter seasonal zones. The line is marked WNA. *See also* **load line zone.**

winter North Atlantic timber freeboard   distance between the deck line and the appropriate load line for a ship with a deck cargo of timber in one of the North Atlantic winter seasonal zones. *See also* **freeboard** *and* **load line zone.**

winter North Atlantic timber load line   line painted on the sides of a ship which shows the maximum depth to which that ship's hull may be immersed when in one of the North Atlantic winter seasonal zones with a deck cargo of timber. The line is marked LWNA. *See also* **load line zone.**

winter timber freeboard   distance between the deck line and the appropriate load line for a ship with a deck cargo of timber in a winter zone. *See also* **freeboard** *and* **load line zone.**

winter timber load line   line painted on the sides of a ship which shows the maximum depth to which that ship's hull may be immersed when in a winter zone with a deck cargo of timber. The line is marked LW. *See also* **load line zone.**

w.i.p.o.n.   *see* **whether in port or not** *above.*

withdraw a ship from the service of charterers (to)   to remove control of a ship from the time charterer for the remaining period of the charter. This action is taken by the shipowner in accordance with the charter when there has been a serious breach of contract, commonly when the charterer has failed to pay hire money on time.

w/m   *see* **weight or measure(ment)** *above.*

W.N.A.   Winter North Atlantic.

w.o.g.   without guarantee. This term is often found in telexes or cables containing details of ships offered on time charter and qualifies, for example, the speed of the ship, designating that this figure is given without commitment.

work to finish (to)   to continue to load or discharge the cargo of a ship after the normal working hours and customary overtime of the port until the balance of the cargo has been completely loaded or discharged. The extra cost of this operation is generally less than the running cost or hire money incurred if the ship waits until the following working day to complete.

153

workable hatch   term in a voyage charter which determines the number of days allowed for loading and/or discharging, by dividing the quantity of cargo in the largest hatch by the quantity per workable hatch per day as stipulated in the charter-party. Difficulties of interpretation may arise in the calculation of laytime allowed when expressed in this way, particularly if the ship has hatches capable of being worked by two gangs simultaneously. Also referred to as a **working hatch.**

working day   day when normal working is carried out in a port.

working day of 24 consecutive hours   working day which equates to one layday. The word consecutive was introduced after it was ruled in court that a working day of 24 hours might be considered as more than one layday according to the length of normal working time each day in a port.

working day of 24 hours   period of time which contains 24 normal working hours. If it is the custom of a port that eight hours represents the normal working time per day, then a working day of 24 hours would be considered as three laydays.

working hatch   *see* **workable hatch** *above.*

working time saved   charter-party term used to define one method by which despatch money is calculated, that is, by deducting laytime used from laytime allowed. If, for example, a charter-party provides for six laydays for loading and the charterer uses $2\frac{1}{2}$ days, he is entitled to $3\frac{1}{2}$ days' despatch money. Also referred to as **laytime saved.** *See* **all time saved** *for an alternative method of calculating despatch money.*

Worldscale   widely used scale by means of which tanker freights are quoted. Its purpose is to enable shipowners to compare more easily the returns on alternative voyages. The figure 100 (prefixed by W) is allocated to a hypothetical return per ton of cargo using a ship of 19,500 tonnes deadweight on each of a number of standard routes and, for each route, is equivalent to a value in U.S. Dollars. If, for example, W100 = $10 and a shipowner negotiates for $11, he will quote W110. Similarly, if a rate of $9 is required, W90 will be quoted.

w.p.   *see* **weather permitting** *above.*

w.t.s.   *see* **working time saved** *above.*

w.w.d.   *see* **weather working day** *above.*

w.w.r.   *see* **when where ready** *above.*

w.w.r.c.d.   when where ready on completion of discharge. *See under* **when where ready** *above.*

Y

yard   frequently used short form for shipyard, the place where ships are built.

yaw (to)   said of a ship, to fail to steer a straight course.

York–Antwerp Rules   set of rules, agreed upon and amended at several international conventions, which governs general average, what losses are allowable, who is required to contribute and the method of calculating the loss. These rules have not been given the force of law but are incorporated into many contracts of carriage by agreement of the parties.